SWING THE CLUBHEAD

Other books in the
Golf Digest Classic Series
Golf Fundamentals by Seymour Dunn
The Complete Golfer by Harry Vardon
Five Lessons by Ben Hogan

SWING THE CLUBHEAD

BY

ERNEST JONES

America's Foremost Golf Teacher

AS TOLD TO

DAVID EISENBERG

Illustrated with photographs and drawings

ECHO POINT BOOKS & MEDIA, LLC
BRATTLEBORO, VERMONT.

Published in 2017 by Echo Point Books & Media
Brattleboro, Vermont
www.EchoPointBooks.com

Originally published in 1952

Swing the Clubhead
ISBN: 978-1-62654-561-8 (paperback)

Cover design by Justine McFarland

Cover images (*left to right*):

"Frank Arthur Cooper", John Oxley Library,
State Library of Queensland. Taken September, 1937

(no title given) By woodypino, courtesy of Pixabay

"Excited Golfer Cheering on Putting Green on a Foggy Day at the
Golf Course" by wavebreakmedia, courtesy of Shutterstock,
www.shutterstock.com

CONTENTS

FOREWORD

ONE JUNE SUNDAY in 1951 I had, as a sports writer for the *New York Journal-American,* the pleasant assignment of "covering" a golf match between two of the world's most famous women professionals—Miss Patty Berg and Mrs. Babe Didrikson Zaharias. I asked Ernest Jones to accompany me.

He was dubious, at first, so we left the decision to be made the morning of the match. I had to see him at his charming home because we were working on the book. When this Sunday arrived—one of the season's most beautiful, following almost a week of rain—Ernest felt the urge to mingle with the golf crowd.

Characteristically, Ernest pinned a flower in the lapel of his jacket, a rose from his own garden. He placed hat jauntily on head and reached for his cane.

We were off for Deepdale, one of Long Island's famous golf courses. Upon our arrival, we saw a crowd around the practice tee. We joined them. Mrs. Zaharias was practicing her wood shots. Ernest watched the famous Babe for a few minutes and then shook his head.

I was curious to learn what criticism he could make

about a great golfer who was the only member of her sex compared with men in discussions about long hitting. Before he could tell me he was swooped upon by Miss Helen Hicks, 1931 women's champion who now is a famous professional.

This was a grand reunion between old friends who soon were joined by other old friends. The group mingled with the gallery when the match was about to begin. As they strolled along the fairway, the subject, as is inevitable when Ernest Jones is present, became that of swinging a club. The talk started Miss Hicks to reminiscing:

"I'll never forget the 1933 women's championship. Virginia Van Wie and I were the finalists. We also were roommates.

"Virginia was playing poorly and only her putting saved her from being worse than two down at the end of the morning round. I was very confident of victory.

"But something happened in the afternoon. Virginia won four straight holes and went on to a 4 and 3 victory.

"Well, the match and the ceremonies were over. We went out and enjoyed ourselves with many of our friends. It was late when Virginia and I finally reached our room.

"You know how roommates are, and how they talk. No sooner was the door closed than I blurted:

" 'Look. I should have beaten you badly today. I was hitting much better. But you won. Now tell me, what happened?'

"Virginia looked at me a moment. Then she said:

" 'I really don't know.'

" 'Then what were you thinking about?' I demanded.

" 'I thought only about one thing,' said Virginia. 'Swing. Just swing the clubhead.' "

Miss Hicks laughed.

"That," she said, "was Ernest Jones. He had been telling her that for days. So she thought only about swinging, while I thought about everything but swinging—hit this way and that, place the ball, direction. And she beat me for the championship."

Shortly after the Weathervane playoff between Miss Berg and Mrs. Zaharias ended, the latter joined the group. Miss Hicks made the introductions.

"I've heard so very much about you, Mr. Jones," said Mrs. Zaharias.

"I wish you would come to see me one day," said Ernest. "We have much to talk about."

"Yes," said Mrs. Zaharias, "we have. I think you can help me. All I do while on the course is to keep experimenting."

"I know," said Ernest, who still speaks with a decided British accent. "I watched you. The day you can stop experimenting is the day when you will be a very great golfer, maybe the greatest of all."

Only an Ernest Jones could have said that to the woman whom many consider the greatest golfer her sex has produced. There is no questioning that Mrs. Zaharias hits a golf ball further than any woman who ever lived. And yet she and Ernest Jones were agreed on one fact—there was something wrong with the way she hits a golf ball.

Later, Ernest explained it very briefly. It's in her swing. Somewhere along the way, she went off in her swing.

Swing! That is Ernest Jones' teaching credo. It has been his credo for more than thirty years.

His constant reiteration of the one fact, the casting away of all other embellishments which seem to have attached themselves to golf teaching, like leeches, has resulted in his becoming the most famous teacher of golf in America.

I was attracted to Jones because I needed an understanding of the swing. I became one of his many ardent admirers because he reduces his teaching to such simplicity. His down-to-earthness, the homely comparisons with which he explains his theories make it easy to understand him.

There was the time someone said to him:

"You say the swing is everything and that you can feel the swing only through your hands. What I want to know is, HOW do you get to feel the swing through your hands?"

Jones' answer was characteristic:

"It's not HOW you feel, but WHAT you feel. Here, take this tack. Put it on the chair and sit on it. What would you feel if you did? I know how you would feel. Terrible, and in great pain."

Ben Hogan, in a discussion after he scored a 68 at Seminole recently, said much the same thing about the feel of golf:

"I never know why I hit the ball well. I just know when I'm doing it."

Although no club has claimed him as its professional since 1943, when he was at Women's National Golf and Tennis Club, Ernest Jones' fame as a teacher grows steadily. Day after day you will find other teachers and writers quoting him, or referring to his theories.

The United States Golf Association *Journal* used a series of two articles by him during the Winter of 1950. The Professional Golfers' Association made him the principal speaker at its annual convention in November, 1950. For a full afternoon, Jones discussed his golf theories before an audience of the nation's leading professionals. The *Professional Golfer,* monthly magazine of the P.G.A., reported his talk in three installments which spread over seventeen pages.

This is the man who is the golf-teaching counterpart to the man who built a better mousetrap and knew that the world would beat a path to his door. The world of perplexed golfers, from duffers through professionals, beats a path to his door, which is on the seventh floor of the A. G. Spalding Company retail store at Fifth Avenue and 43d Street, in New York City.

In many parts of the golf world he is quickly recognized because of the repeated reprinting of photographs showing him explaining his golf principles by swinging a jackknife which hangs from a string.

Ernest Jones' golf career began as a small boy in England, near Manchester. He won his first caddie's prize, a fourth, at the age of nine. He won first prize the next three years. He became the assistant professional at the Chislehurst Golf Club in 1905, at the tender age of eighteen. (In 1949 the same club made him an honorary member.) He earned the job as much because he was a capable maker of clubs as he was a good golfer.

Jones attracted considerable attention because he promised to develop into a great golfer. That he was, instead, steered into becoming a great teacher can be attributed to World War I.

He won the Kent Cup, a tournament similar in importance to a sectional professional championship here, in 1914. He won it again in 1920, a remarkable feat for reasons which will be explained.

Even then, Jones realized there was something wrong with the teaching of golf.

"From my first effort as a teacher I realized that I had not the slightest idea of how to go about it," he reminisced. "Something had to be done. I decided that my best course was to begin a careful study of books on how to teach. I read every book by every leading professional.

"I must confess, however, that with a single exception the books failed to help me. They merely added to my confusion because of their many contradictions. I did not then appreciate all that was talked about was the reaction to an action which could not be photographed."

The exception was a book published in 1887 and titled: "The Art of Golf," by Sir Walter Simpson.

"That book started me to thinking along a line entirely different from anything I had encountered up to this time," said Jones. "It emphasized that in golf 'there is one categorical imperative. Hit the ball. But there are no minor absolutes.'"

Jones' search for a better understanding of teaching golf was interrupted in January, 1915, when he joined the British Army. In November he was sent to France where, in the fighting around Loos the following March, he was so badly wounded that he lost his right leg, just below the knee. Sixteen pieces of shrapnel had lodged in his leg, right forearm and in his head.

Yet, only four months later, the newspapers reported a remarkable event. Ernest Jones had shot an 83 on the Royal Norwich links while playing on one leg. Jones went out in 38, but he tired badly and scored a 45 for the second nine.

The day Ernest shot his 83 was his first out of the hospital. It was the first time he had walked on crutches, using them to walk to the ball, but balancing himself on one leg when he addressed the ball and swung the club.

What Jones remembers best about that round of golf is that Arthur Havers, who later became British champion, had given him a stroke a hole handicap. When he went out in 38 it became no contest.

On that first attempt, Jones discovered he couldn't use the wood clubs for long shots. They were too long for him to control the swing while perched on one leg. Instead, he used a ladies no. 1 iron. But he adjusted himself so rapidly to playing on one leg that shortly afterwards he shot a 72 on the Clacton course, which was a long one. He shot a 70 his first week at Chislehurst. When he won the Kent Cup for the second time in 1920, he was using an artificial leg.

How did he do it? Small in stature, at only 5 feet

13

5½ inches, and then weighing less than 130 pounds, he was capable of shooting a 70 with one leg—a most phenominal feat.

Jones explains it simply. The swing. He always hit the ball with an ease which was conspicuous. Daryn Hammond, an English writer who became so intrigued by his teachings that he wrote a book called: "The Golf Swing: the Ernest Jones Method," said:

"In his use of the hands and the fingers he resembled Vardon. But his swing was flatter and rather more compact. It was accompanied by less suggestion of power, but perhaps even greater suggestion of speed."

Mr. Hammond's compliment of writing such a book, as long ago as 1920, indicated that even in his youth Jones was recognized by his fellow craftsmen as a golfer who brought to the sport a most penetrating mind.

"He was known as a player of original views," said Mr. Hammond, "a player who satisfied himself about the mechanics of the swing, and who played the game fully conscious of what he was doing and why he was doing it."

Jones commands the same admiration today. As proof, I need but quote from the Professional Golfer of February, 1951:

"We feel Mr. Jones' theories are among the most thought-provoking ever placed before golf professionals."

DAVID EISENBERG

Brooklyn, N. Y.
February, 1952.

14

INTRODUCTION

THE FIRST BOOK about my theories of teaching golf was written in 1920. This one is the third. The 32 intervening years have convinced me more than ever that golf is easy to learn once you properly understand and have fixed in your mind the fundamental principle of the swing:

"There is only one categorical imperative in golf, and that is to hit the ball. There are no minor absolutes."

The above quotation from Sir Walter Simpson's remarkable book is, from cause to effect, golf.

Learn it, understand it and, if you are a beginner, you are on the right road to good golfing. If you are a more expert player snared in the complexities of attempting to remember at one and the same time the stiff left arm, head down, braced leg, right arm pressed to side, etc., etc., you are started on the road to escape from the Minotaur's labyrinth of confusion.

The teaching of golf has become overwhelmed in paralysis through analysis.

I am as convinced today, as I was in 1920, that the golf swing can be readily taught, and consistently per-

15

formed, BUT ONLY IF IT IS CONCEIVED AS ONE MOVEMENT.

That is the only way to become a good golfer. By carrying a clear mental picture of the swing as being one movement you will insure the coordination of all the members of the body, especially the shoulders. The body and all its parts should be TREATED AS DISASTROUS LEADERS BUT AS WHOLLY ADMIRABLE FOLLOWERS OF THE ACTION OF THE HANDS AND FINGERS.

Forget about everything else. You cannot do more than one thing at a time. So don't let your mind and actions flitter.

The basic action of the swing is the PROPER ACTION OF THE HANDS AND FINGERS.

It is through their proper use that you will acquire the proper swing. You MUST rid yourself of the distraction of trying to think about all those things against which most golfers are warned. You do not have the time in the fraction of a second between taking the club back and returning it to contact with the ball.

Keep your left arm straight . . . Twist your hips . . . Pivot . . . Cock your wrists . . . Get your left heel off the ground . . . Clamp your right heel INTO the ground . . . Tuck chin beneath left shoulder . . . Keep shoulders on a plane . . . Relax your knees . . . etc., etc. . . . . Now isn't it silly to attempt to think about all those matters in the second or less it takes to swing a club? It cannot be done.

The sooner you understand that you swing the clubhead with your hands, that from this cause comes automatically the effect of making all the correct body movements, the nearer you will be to the perfect swing. And perfection is achieved, finally, not when there is no longer anything to add, but when there is no longer anything to take away.

Those were my thoughts 32 years ago. They are, to-day, my theory of teaching golf. Thus, this book can be considered a successor to Daryn Hammond's "The Golf Swing: the Ernest Jones Method," and the book which I wrote in collaboration with Innis Brown in 1936, called "Swinging into Golf."

In this new book I am making available to the golfer hungering to break 100, anxious to rise from the vast class of the duffer, all the new knowledge I acquired from my contact with the many students who, while I was attempting to help them, advanced my own golf education.

When teaching golf I attempt to create the picture of the fundamental principle which applies to all golfers. I repeat:

"To hit the ball.

"There is one categorical imperative, but no minor absolutes."

What Sir Walter Simpson inspired in me when I first read his book, I have been teaching ever since.

The loss of my right leg confirmed to me the fundamental truth that the stroke must be regarded as one complete action. You initiate it by swinging the club. Because I followed the basic tenets of the swing, I discovered I could still play good golf, even on one leg.

17

Playing on one leg disproved the emphasis which so many still place on body pivot.

The teachers who devote themselves to details consider golf a science. It is not. Golf is an art. Those who think in terms of golf being a science have, unfortunately, tried to part from each other the arms, the head, the shoulder, the body, the hips and the legs. They make the golfer a worm cut into bits with each part wriggling in every-which-way direction.

I try to eliminate all other considerations and to concentrate on one principle, the art of swinging the clubhead.

I have no quarrel with those who delight in analyzing the successive movements of different parts of the anatomy during the course of a stroke. Many of us are curious to take a watch apart to see what makes it tick. To quote Sir Walter Simpson:

"The average golfer must be allowed to theorize to some extent. It is a necessary concession to him as a thinking animal. . . . On the other hand, if he does not recognize hitting the ball as his main business, and theory as his recreation, he becomes so bad a player that he nearly gives it up."

I depart from Sir Walter's advice in one respect. I prefer the word "swing," where he says "hit." I prefer "swing the clubhead," to "hit the ball" because there is a vast difference between swinging at a ball and hitting at a ball. You must swing to hit successfully. One of my many pupils recently wrote me as follows:

"As for the swing, I have come to a knowledge of it, but how many others have? Perhaps one in a hundred.

18

I realize how difficult, almost impossible, it is to teach a feeling. But until one gets it, he has nothing definite.

"A hit is one of the most indefinite things in golf. It is sometimes yes and sometimes no. A swing is definite. It is a totality.

"I have insisted on swing with those I try to help and it is a matter of coming back to it, minute by minute, and hour by hour. A hit in golf is like a Latin sentence without a verb. The swing is the very verb. That's the substance, and how it hides! It is a shame how swing has been hidden. It is such a simple thing."

There are more ways than one of hitting. There is only one way to swing. The swing is everything. To strike the ball with power it is necessary to move the clubhead faster. But you cannot move the clubhead faster than you can swing it.

I claim nothing new or revolutionary in "swing the clubhead," because the term is used to describe the player's effort to wield the club. It is used whether or not it bears a resemblance to a true swing, by virtually every duffer who steps onto a golf course.

If the golf teacher can make the pupil understand the simplicity of the swing, he will pass on the formula which makes playing easy. So very few understand, much less can explain, just what is meant by swinging the clubhead.

I asked "what is a swing?" of a number of leading golfers during a discussion of a famous player's so-called "swing." The answer came:

"That can mean anything."

19

"That," I said, "is one of golf's tragedies. It should mean everything."

There you have what I believe to be the problem in teaching others. Swing sounds so simple. It is—so simple that it is too difficult for hundreds of thousands of golfers to comprehend. It is so simple that it is difficult to induce many pupils to accept it.

Thus, I have to be repetitious, both when I teach individual pupils and in my writing. There is no other way of assuring satisfactory results. This book will consist of constant repetition. I shall beg the indulgence of those who feel I am overdoing it.

Good golf is easy. And easy golf is enjoyable golf. It is tragic that so many make of it such labor.

If I can help a few of golf's great army of laborers to become players, I shall feel highly repaid for my efforts.

ERNEST JONES

Glen Head, L.I.
February, 1952.

PHOTOGRAPHIC SECTION

THE SWING IS EVERY-THING—*The author, Ernest Jones, had beautiful form which was widely appreciated even in his youth. You can catch the ease and freedom of his stroking from the finish of the iron shots shown on this page. At the right, he is seen playing before World War I. He lost the lower part of his right leg as a British soldier during the war. He continued playing, however, and you can see the same excellent form pictured above. Daryn Hammond, an English writer, said then about Mr. Jones: "His swing was accompanied by less suggestion of power, but perhaps even greater suggestion of speed."*

GOOD GOLF IS EASY—You need no further proof than the pictures of Diane Wilson, taken when she was 5½ years of age. At her age Diane can swing so beautifully because she does not let her imagination interfere with the feel of the clubhead. She has shot a 71 for nine holes and her father, a well-known professional, is now entering her in junior tournaments. Diane makes golf look easy because it is easy. See Chapter One.

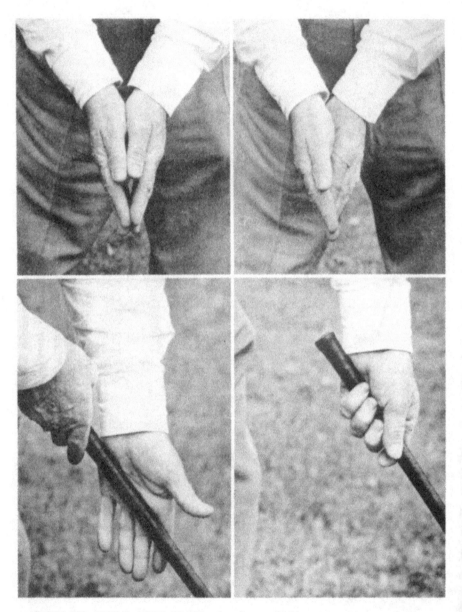

HOW TO HOLD THE CLUB—*On this and the next page are shown the successive steps in the proper method of holding the club. I recommend the overlapping grip as the best. Correct hand position is most*

important. A simple routine for success is to bring the palms of the hands together. Then place the right hand above the left as shown. Now take the club. Place left hand (see lower left picture on opposite page) on shaft. Notice (lower right) position of thumb and forefinger. Now place right hand on shaft as shown (above left). Notice how pinkie of right hand laps over forefinger of left (above right). Also note position of thumb and forefinger in same picture. To the right you see position of hands when ready to swing the club. See how both thumbs extend diagonally across shaft, how thumbs and forefingers are in a position to do the job. See Chapter Three.

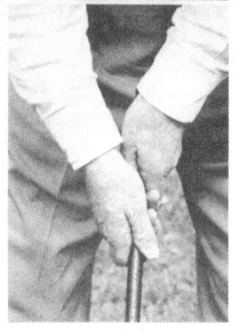

HOW TO ADDRESS THE BALL—*The three general stances are closed (above left), open (above right) and square (opposite page). I recommend the square. Notice the position of ease and comfort when addressing*

ball, which lies midway between the two feet. With the proper stance you can attain that position of balance at rest so vital to good golf. See Chapter Four.

THE SWING—*Whatever your hands take hold of, they must have control of. Proper action of the hands and fingers is the basis of the swing. Begin with the correct grip and stance (above left). Notice (above right) that the hands remain firmly in control at the start of the backswing, with the body responding automatically*

to their action. The hands are still firmly in control at the top of the backswing (below left). They are still doing their job at the finish (below right). See Chapter Five.

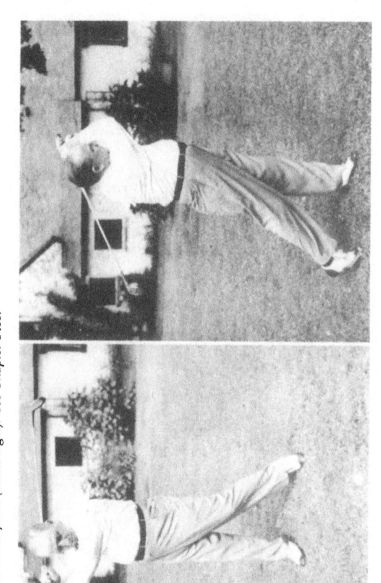

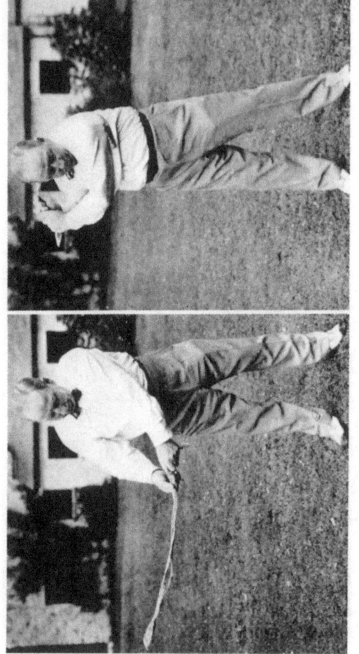

HOW TO ACQUIRE A SWING—*The swing must be conceived as one continuous motion. The gadget pictured on these two pages proves that fundamental. My jackknife tied to the end of a handkerchief, being flexible, cannot transmit power. Only the hands do that. And if the hands are not used to create a swinging*

motion it is impossible to succeed in going through the motions, as in swinging a club. With this gadget you can learn what is meant by the phrase that the good golfer has, at all times, the feel of what he is doing with the clubhead. Remember: there is only one swing. That is the correct one. See Chapter Seven.

TIMING AND RHYTHM—Swinging the club and my jackknife simultaneously *is a test of the swing. When I swing properly the jackknife will follow the clubhead as seen below. When I fail to swing properly, the clubhead will move back but the knife will not. See Chapter Eight.*

OBSTACLES TO SWINGING—*The greatest obstacle is pressure in any form. The photographs below show once again how the jackknife follows the clubhead in the proper swing (left). When, however, I use leverage (pressure) the result is what you see at the right. See Chapter Ten.*

THE PUTTER—*The great Byron Nelson said: "I am completely unaware of making any attempt to swing one club differently than another." This is true with the putter as with any other club. A swing is a positive, indivisible motion backward and forward. A short putt takes the same measure of time to complete as does a full drive if the same length of club is used. Thus, the longer the swing, as in driving, the greater the force. The shorter, as in putting, the lesser the force. Notice, in the pictures at the left, that the hands are in full control of the swing with the putter. See Chapter Nine.*

WOODS AND IRONS—*The swing never changes, though the length of its arc does, according to the shot. The difference in the clubs takes care of the rest. See Chapter Nine.*

MENTAL HAZARDS—*Thinking about the legs, hips or other parts of the body is a mental hazard. The hands do the job. I prove it by hitting while sitting. See Chapter Eleven.*

SWING THE CLUBHEAD

GOOD GOLF IS EASY

I HAVE SAID that golf is easy. I offer as proof the sequence of photographs in the picture section, showing a five-year-old girl swinging a club. Stop right here and turn to a study of those pictures. Devote some time to them, at least as much time as it will take you to read this chapter.

Certainly, that child hasn't the adult intelligence to know the how and what of her swing. But she has the ability to feel what she is doing. The result is that this baby swings the club with an ease which is the envy of 999 out of 1,000 adults who play golf. Nowhere, not even in a U. S. Open championship, will you see more perfect form.

If a five-year-old child can learn to swing, there is no reason on earth why you cannot. All you need do is to repeat the action of that child. She was not distracted in her swing. Her mind was not cluttered by the countless don'ts which fill the air whenever people talk golf. She merely took the club as it should be taken, in her two hands, and did with it what comes naturally. She swung.

When you are part of a gallery watching great stars, what is the most common expression you hear around you? Isn't it:

"They sure make it look easy."

Yes, they do make it look easy—because golf is easy.

You may be a hacker who struggles around golf courses weekend after weekend without ever breaking a hundred. But haven't there been times when you got off the perfect shot? And weren't you surprised that you hardly felt any strain from the use of power? That was because, for once perhaps, you were swinging.

And if you can swing the club once, you can do it again. When you understand the principles of the swing, which I hope to pass on to you in this book, you should be able to swing that way again and again and again.

I am reminded of a letter I received from a friend who teaches in the South. He was teaching a woman. The more he tried to pass on to her the simplicity of the swing, the more difficulty he encountered.

He almost gave up in despair. Then he noticed a young caddie swinging a club. He had a beautiful swing. In sudden inspiration, he called the caddie, teed up a ball and ordered him to swing. The caddie hit ball after ball straight down the middle of the fairway, for some 200 yards. The woman sat in amazement. Then she spoke up.

"May I ask the boy a question?" Then turning to the caddie, she said, "What were you thinking about when you hit the ball?"

"Nothing," said the caddie.

That did it. Obviously, the woman had cluttered her mind with all the don'ts which have been cast at every person who attempted golf. She decided to think of "nothing," and her progress as a golfer was accelerated.

I can quote one great golfer after another about the simplicity of the game of golf. Unfortunately, many of those professionals, who learned the proper swing as teen-age caddies, have not learned the principles of teaching what they practice.

Bobby Jones, considered by many experts the greatest golfer of all time, had this to say:

"The one idea for the golfer to keep always in his mind is that, when playing a shot, his job is to SWING the clubhead. If he does this, hitting the ball will take care of itself. And the place to start SWINGING is at the very beginning, as soon as the movement of the stroke gets under way.

"The hands form the connecting links by which the forces brought to life in the player's body are transmitted to the club."

The great Ben Hogan, who twice won the U. S. Open championship after suffering a near-fatal automobile accident, said:

"Instead of trying to maneuver the ball with your body, arms and hands, trust your swing and the club you select for the shot."

Byron Nelson said:

"Many golfers add unnecessary complexity to the game by feeling that they must use a different swing for each club in the bag. This is incorrect. I am completely unaware of making any attempt to swing one club differently than another."

Joe Novak, the president of the Professional Golfers' Association, has said:

"Fundamentally, good golf instruction means cutting out complications. The rest is embellishment."

However, the quotation which reduces to the simplest terms the reason why golf should be easy to play, is from Sam Snead. Said he:

"I play the shots in the most simple way I know how."

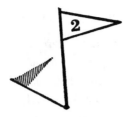

MY THEORY OF TEACHING

First, I wish to emphasize that there are no secrets to golf. The secret of success is practice, constant but intelligent practice. There are fundamental laws which we must follow.

In this book, as in my teaching, only one lesson is taught. Each chapter is a restatement, from different angles, of the principle of golf as I believe it. It is that the one factor which makes good golf possible is the swing.

The swing. After all these years of teaching I must say, regretfully, that the average golfer has little understanding of what he calls "my swing."

THE SWING IS THE ACTION OF MOVING A GOLF CLUB TO CREATE THE MOST PERFECT MOTION WHEN STRIKING THE BALL.

To the average golfer every type of motion is called "my swing." He uses the term loosely, even incorrectly. And yet, to most, swing is virgin territory seldom explored.

In this chapter, I want to explain why I insist that learning to swing the clubhead is the one essential in laying the foundation for good golf. By learning to swing you will develop consistently the skill which makes it a joy to play this royal and ancient game.

I have already repeated that in golf there is only one categorical imperative—"hit the ball,"—and that there are no minor absolutes. I want to go one step further with that thought.

THERE IS ONLY ONE THING YOU ARE PERMITTED TO USE IN STRIKING THE BALL—THE CLUBHEAD.

To hit the ball effectively that clubhead must be moved in a manner which will develop the greatest force at the moment it strikes the ball.

The greatest force you can develop with a given amount of power is centrifugal in nature. It is achieved by swinging. It is not necessary to quote from the science of physics for proof. Even ancient men understood that a swinging action developed maximum force. Remember David and Goliath and think: how did David get the force into the stone?

You can transmit your power to the clubhead through only one medium—the hands with which you hold the club, not the legs, the shoulders or other parts. The hands function in the action of stroking while the rest of the body responds wholly to the initiating action of swinging the clubhead with the hands and fingers.

I repeat, because this principle must be carefully digested so that you will understand it. As a doctor pupil of mine once remarked:

"What you are teaching is like the food you eat. First it must be swallowed. Then it must be digested. But it does no good until it has been assimilated."

The club is held in the hands—largely in the fingers—and everything the golfer does with the club is done through them. It is through the hands that he gains the feel of the club. The hands are the medium through which power is transmitted to the clubhead. "Touch" is entirely in the hands and fingers. The fingers impart to the blow the life and vitality which make the ball travel.

Most poor golfers merely use their hands to hold the club. They do not understand that it is through the hands and fingers alone that they can influence the behavior of the club.

Why do so many golfers fail to understand this basic principle? They are too intent on trying to remember to keep the left arm straight, the right elbow in close to the side; to take a full pivot and cock the wrists at the top of the backswing; keep the head still, brace the left side at impact and follow through after hitting the ball. I might add, and so on, ad nauseam.

Yes, you do most of the above when you hit properly. But all are incidental to the action of swinging the clubhead. It is cause, swinging through the use of the hands, which produces the effect, the subconscious carrying out of the above-mentioned details without thinking about them. The latter are wholly responsive to your conscious effort in wielding the club through the use of the hands. To every action there is a natural reaction.

As for learning by observation, which should be the natural way, unfortunately that which the adult onlooker sees is not sensed in the same way by the performer. One uses his sense of sight, the other his sense of feel.

Let us consider the action of swinging. The simplest

31

example of a swing is that of the pendulum in an old grandfather's clock. There is little in the swing of the pendulum which suggests speed. But remember, the pendulum moves through a comparatively short arc. Gradually extend that arc into a complete circle. Can you appreciate the increased speed of the swing as the arc is extended?

Just as the rod swings the pendulum, so do the hands swing the clubhead, not the body. The swinging club, through the hands, finds its own center. Whether the swing moves through a short arc, for putting, or a long one, for driving, the force is applied in the same manner. The resultant action, in moving the object swung, has the same characteristics. The pivot, about which you hear so much, is the RESULT of swinging, not the CAUSE.

Although a circle consists of 360 degrees, you never would think of drawing one by piecing together 360 tiny arcs. You draw one line with one continuous motion.

It is the same in swinging. The stroke is one single action of swinging the clubhead. You must create a mental pattern of this fact. Any other conception of the stroke— as a series of separate actions to each of which you must give your conscious attention—is impossible to attain.

It is through the medium of the hands and fingers that you control any tool. In golf, the club is your tool. To exert control, you must have power. Try using a hammer by letting it drop without force. It will be harder to control. In developing the considerable force of swinging the club properly, the various parts of the body will respond with the proper movements.

Unfortunately, most golfers persist in thinking about

32

how to get their power INTO the stroke, rather than of USING their power to create force in the clubhead. Your power is the strength and energy which you already have.

Balance, which simply is an even distribution of static weight, is a factor in the necessary movement of the body. Balance at rest is when you stand evenly on your feet. Balance in motion is when you walk. Try both. Notice how, in neither case, are you conscious of any effort to maintain balance, which is dynamic and not static. This will be described in another chapter.

Before you begin your swing you are in a condition of static balance. You are in a condition of balance at rest. As you begin to move the club back, you develop a condition of balance in motion. The transition from one to the other is no more complicated than starting to walk from a standing position. But you create complications when you regard, as objectives in themselves, the successive changes in body position, brought on by the movement.

I am reminded, when watching a golfer suffer the tortures of paralyzing himself in his attempts at self-analysis, of the following jingle:

A centipede was happy quite, until a toad in fun,
Said "Pray which leg goes after which?"
This put his mind in such a fix,
He fell distracted in a ditch,
Considering how to run.

It is just as logical to assume an easy, comfortable position for starting a golf stroke as it is in initiating any other kind of action. After assuming the easy, comfortable position, you must hold the club in the proper manner. With that club in your hands you must stand in a position which will permit swinging the club in a way that will propel the ball in the direction desired.

The proper method of holding the club and the stance are subjects for future chapters. Here I wish to emphasize that, given the proper position in starting the stroke, body balance becomes spontaneous so long as you concentrate on swinging the clubhead.

One of my prize pupils was Miss Virginia Van Wie, the National women's champion in 1932, 1933 and 1934. After she won her first championship she said to me:

"I am getting such a big kick out of my golf ever since I stopped trying to do all the things I was supposed to do and began to concentrate simply on swinging the clubhead. Now all my late helpers tell me how well I am doing the things they have been trying to get me to do for years."

After winning her third championship, Miss Van Wie said:

"Every time I leave you I think I know exactly what a swing is all about. But every time I come back I get a better conception of it."

It proves that although I am devoting an entire book to teaching one subject—the swing—you cannot become too perfect in that single enterprise. You can hope only to approach closer and closer to that perfection.

You will reach it if you learn to understand exactly what is meant by swinging and then acquiring, through patient and diligent application, a true swinging action through the sense of touch, or "feel."

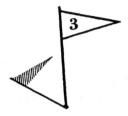

HOW TO HOLD THE CLUB

I PREFER THE WORD "hold" to "grip," although the latter is in almost universal usage. The word "grip" connotes a hold with a viselike tensity, which is a decided handicap.

I believe the word subconsciously causes you to grasp the club so hard that it destroys your ability to wield it properly. However, because of its wide use, I shall have to use "grip" at times.

The manner in which the club is held is of the greatest importance because the proper hold is essential to the proper swing. Remember, you swing through the hands. Whether your tool is a hammer or a golf club, how you hold it must be suited to the manner in which it is to be used. Only thus can the best results be obtained.

There are many ways of holding the club. But first: why do you hold the club? Obviously, to enable you to have authority over it. It must be in such a way that you can use both hands as a unit. There is, obviously, more power in two hands than in one, so long as both are used for the same purpose. And since the principle finger of either hand is the thumb, so must it be used to the best advantage for control and speed.

There are three general types of holds, or grips: the *overlap,* in widest use; the *interlock* and the so-called *natural.*

In the overlapping grip, the thumb of the left hand extends diagonally across the shaft. The pad of the thumb of the right hand rests on the shaft. The little finger of the right hand is lapped over the forefinger of the left hand, hence the name. See picture section.

In the interlocking grip, the thumb of the left hand extends across the shaft back of the right hand. The little finger of the right hand and the forefinger of the left hand are interlocked in such a manner that the tip of the left forefinger is pressed to the ridge between the knuckles of the third and little fingers on the right hand. The tip of the right hand's little finger presses on the knuckle of the left hand.

In the natural grip, the two hands are free from interlocking or overlapping. The fingers of the one hand are in the same relative position on one side of the club shaft as are the fingers of the other hand on the reverse side of the shaft. This grip is more commonly known as the baseball grip. It is rarely used because, though it has power, it lacks flexibility or "touch."

So long as the two hands work as a unit any grip can be effective. I even know a number of cross-handed golfers who play well.

Yet I reject the interlocking grip. It interferes with the full use of the left forefinger and thumb, most important in the proper holding and swinging of the club.

The overlapping grip, used by the great majority of golfers, is the one I favor and recommend. It has all the qualities and none of the failings of the other grips. In this grip, the thumbs and first fingers of the two hands, which do the job and sense the feel of the club, have the contact with the shaft, which is vital.

The drawings on this and the following page show the correct method of placing the hands on the club.

In holding the club it is necessary to grip firmly enough to assure control throughout the action. Too loose a grip is just as disastrous as one which is too tight. This is as true of holding a golf club as it is of holding a hammer or a pencil.

Try this experiment. Close the fingers of your hand as tightly as possible. Notice how your wrist stiffens, as well as the forearm and upper arm. It is the same when you grip a club too tightly.

Now take a pencil in your hand. Write something. Notice that the pencil is held just firmly enough to guide it lightly over the surface of the paper. You do not clutch the pencil. That would destroy the flexibility and dexterity of the movement of your hand and writing would become a difficult chore. A tight grip is for delivering a heavy blow. In golf, you aim to deliver a swift blow.

Notice also that you hold the pencil with your thumb and forefinger, which also are the leading factors in guiding the movement of the club. The speed which is necessary for wielding the club is generated in those fingers.

The club is placed diagonally across the palm of your

37

left hand, with the thumb and forefinger leading the way in gripping the shaft. Gripping with the palm entirely provides the power which is perfect for tugging a rope. It is not for golf.

Consider further. The thumb is your principal finger. You use it to undo a button. You lift a cup of coffee or tea with the index finger and the thumb. You hold a spoon with thumb and forefinger. You throw a ball or stone, or anything else, with thumb and forefinger. Q.E.D. You hold the club with the thumb and forefinger of the two hands, using the remaining fingers as helpers.

I have already talked about balance. There is a balance of the hands. Hold your hands straight out (see picture section). Bring the palms together. Now place the right hand so that it rests on the left hand. Drop the hands to the position in which you normally hold the club. Close your fingers as if gripping the club.

What do you see? First, the thumb and index finger on each hand form a V which is in direct center. Next, the back of hands face in opposite directions. The palms face each other. They are straight out, and in the correct position in relation to each other.

Take a golf club. Hold the shaft in the same manner. The hands now are in perfect position for wielding the club because they are balanced in the line of flight the ball should follow.

To bounce a ball off the floor, the palm faces straight down. It is upward when bouncing the ball off the ceiling. Since stroking requires movement to the left and then to the right, the palm of the left hand faces to the right, while the palm of the right hand faces to the left.

When looking at your hands as they hold the club you should see the knuckles of the index and second fingers of the left hand, with only the suggestion of the knuckle of the third finger in your range of vision. Only then are your hands in proper position.

I know there are fine golfers with faulty grips. I insist that they play well in spite of their handicap, not because of it. To help you learn to enjoy golfing with ease, I must insist on the correct method.

HOW TO ADDRESS THE BALL

AT THE RISK of someone taunting me with an extremely corny gag about a three-cent stamp, I prefer the above heading to the golf term called "the stance." Fundamentally, this subject also comes under the heading of balance.

Standing properly to the ball is just as vital in assuring an easy, swinging action as is the proper placing of the hands. Where your feet are placed determines the ease with which the body responds during the action of the swing. Their position—in relation to each other and to where the ball rests—fixes the foundation for the action of the stroke.

There are many stances. Golfers use three general types. These are—*open, closed* and *square.* In each case, the term refers to the position of the feet in relation to the ball and the line of flight intended—or hoped for.

The square stance is most commonly used and is the only perfectly balanced position. The toes of both feet are in a line parallel with the line of play. In the open stance, the left foot is drawn back slightly. In the closed stance, the left foot is forward. Experts use all three, to serve various purposes.

But it is not the stance which makes or breaks a golfer. It merely is a step toward good golf, though one or the other of the stances have been in fashion at various times because of outstanding success by some individual star. One also can play very bad golf with one or the other of these stances.

There is more to the stance, much more. A prime requisite is the balanced body already mentioned and which is necessary to proper swinging of the club. A balanced body is a free body. It is a failing of many golfers to think of the swinging of the club as one thing and the balance of the body as another. Such golfers tend to seek balance by clamping the feet to the ground and spreading them wide apart. The intelligent golfer should sense the error of such a position because of the feeling of a locked body which is the result of legs spread too wide apart.

The stance should provide a feeling of ease and comfort, with the posture allowing the body to yield easily to the action of swinging. There should be no tenseness or resistance. When addressing the ball you should glow from the feeling of easy balance—from side to side and from back to front. Balance will permit the correct response by the body to the swinging of the clubhead as initiated by the hands and fingers.

In addressing the ball you must stand comfortably on your feet. You do not clamp down on your heels. You do not dig your feet into the ground as if bracing for a weight-lifting contest. You do not keel forward on your toes, or go into excessive waggling or jiggling like a victim of St. Vitus Dance. You stand on the soles of your FEET, gripping the turf through the ball, the big toe AND the heel. Balance at rest is simply an even distribution of weight as you address the ball. Balance in motion is a state or condition governed by centrifugal force, when you are swinging.

The free action of the body, legs and feet, all moving in response to the action of the hands, can result only from a balanced position. And a balanced body is an effect of good swinging.

I wish here to inject myself once again, but only to stress my point. My ability to play good golf with only one leg after the first World War proved to me that even one leg is enough to assure proper balance, provided one does the right thing. That right thing is the swing, and in the swing, the sure guide to the feet are the hands.

Ben Hogan could hardly walk after his terrible automobile accident a few years ago. But he had good use of his hands, so he made his brilliant golf comeback to win two straight U. S. Open championships. Patty Berg and Betty Jameson both suffered broken legs, but they came back to resume brilliant golf careers. Fortunately, they had not broken their hands.

There is an unfortunate tendency to measure even to inches the proper spacing of the feet when standing to the ball. There is no scale of measurement. The feet should be as wide apart as is necessary for balance on each shot. It is generally accepted that such balance is best secured by standing with the feet as wide apart as your shoulders for full wood shots. As the shot gets shorter the stance narrows. A stance which is too wide will lock the body and restrict the swing. Too narrow a stance for a full swing will cut down the base of action and throw you off balance.

In teaching beginners, I explain the swing first. Then I tell them where to place their feet. I have found that by learning the proper swing the pupil almost automatically falls into the stance which permits that proper swing.

In taking your position with feet as wide apart as your shoulders, the toes should be pointed naturally. This also is a natural result of proper swinging, because toes pointed naturally permit the body to respond properly to the action of the hands on the upswing, the downswing and the follow through. Thus, if one is naturally pigeon-toed it would be a strain to turn them outward. If one naturally turns his toes outward, as most people do, that becomes the natural position.

In holding the clubhead to the ball, bear in mind the position of SIX O'CLOCK. The clubhead is directly in the middle of your body.

There is no exact measurement to determine how far back you should stand from the ball. The club being used largely determines that. You should be bending forward slightly at the waist, how much is also dependent upon the length of the club.

The legs should be straight, but easy at the knees. Avoid stiffness of the legs.

When taking your position first rest the clubhead behind the ball. Do not stand too far back, nor bend over too much. The body should be reasonably erect. The slight bend mentioned is a natural result of the length of the club. Naturally, you should be free in your movement. For this reason a waggle or two, the preliminary movement of the clubhead back and forth over the ball, are helpful.

Before turning to the next chapter, devote a few more minutes to studying the pictures on the stance.

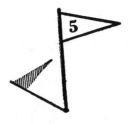

THE SWING

Now WE COME to the meat of this discussion—the swing. It is the swing, and only that, which makes the golfer. Therefore, it follows that the golfer must understand what is a swing.

Quickly now, what is a swing? Can you answer correctly?

A swing is a definite form of motion. Webster devotes considerable space to defining the word. To swing is to have a regular to-and-fro motion, as of a pendulum; to oscillate. Swing, as a noun, is the arc or extent through which an object swings. It also is the force created by something swinging.

Carried over to golf, it is one continuous motion, to and fro, backward and forward, a definite form of motion which must be produced into the clubhead to create the greatest force of which your power is capable. It creates centrifugal force.

Unfortunately, those who have the best swings, seem unable to pass on this information. They know how to swing, but not how to teach the swing. That is why so many fine golfers have been guilty of teaching doctrines which are false.

Describing the swing in words is difficult because it is something which one must feel. It cannot be readily identified by sight. Seeing can help only if you have the feel of the swing. In the hope that you have the feel of the swing I have added to the section of photographs several which may help these words in their appointed task of making you a better golfer.

The basis of the swing is the proper action set up by hands and fingers. It is axiomatic that the only way to have control of the motion of the clubhead is through the medium of the hands and fingers. Thus it is necessary for you to have a clear understanding of how properly to hold a club. If you have not that clear understanding I advise you strongly to re-study Chapter Three on "How to Hold the Club."

The proper grip naturally will help you in your feel of the swing. Holding the club improperly will create difficulties which make it almost impossible to swing.

All golfers today talk about their swing. Unfortunately, to most of them it is non-existent. But, in their misfortunes on the links, they'll ask:

"What is wrong with my swing?"

My answer is "nothing," because their swing is non-existent.

No person can do more than one thing at a time. For that reason I insist that the golf swing can be but one continuous motion, and nothing else.

The form, the shape, of a swing is an arc or part of a circle. As I said before, to make a circle you draw one continuous line, not 360 because there are 360 degrees in a circle. Do you appreciate that? That one line, the golf swing, can be taught only through the use of the hands and fingers.

To be able to swing you must understand this fact. Since you feel the swing and since the hands are the only parts of your body which are in contact with the club, they must be the medium through which the swing becomes possible. You cannot feel the swing with your feet, your shoulders, your hips or your arms.

When a good golfer swings he has, at all times, the feel of what he is doing with the clubhead. He does not see the myriad movements made by the many parts of the body when stroking. He never learned through a detailed analysis of the duties of each part of the body. He learned how to hold the club, how to stand, and he swung. He learned much as a child learns to swing the rope when skipping.

Thus, that good golfer, when addressing the ball, concentrates wholly on his hands, which are holding the club with which he must strike the ball. When he thinks only of hitting the ball with the clubhead through the medium of his hands, has eliminated all the other distractions, he finds that he does well, and that the remaining parts of his body have carried through their allotted duties, although he never gave them a thought.

You are trying to become a good golfer, not a contortionist. You must understand that the various members of the body are normally anxious to get busy too strenuously—and too soon. You must curb this instinct and, as I said before, the only way is to treat them as disas-

47

trous leaders, and as wholly admirable followers. Since the initiative is in the hands and fingers, the moment you properly move the club with the hands, everything else will be set into correct motion.

Try this test as an illustration. Place your hand on a table. Now draw an imaginary circle around your thumb, using your first finger. The thumb is the pivotal point.

When I have my pupils do this, I casually say:

"That wasn't hard. But tell me quickly, what did you do with your thumb."

Three times out of four, the answer is:

"Nothing. I kept the thumb perfectly still."

So I say: "Try it again."

Immediately, the pupil realizes that the thumb *has* to move if it is to act as the pivot. It is impossible for it to remain still.

The same thing happens when you swing the clubhead around your body. Try it and you will see what I mean. Or try this, holding the club as you would a baseball bat. Swing it fast, horizontally, so that the force of the swing carries your body around in a pivot. Isn't the pivot the result of the swing, and not the cause?

I have another device with which I illustrate the swing, a pocket knife attached to a string. I swing the knife and the string is taut because a swinging action always is an expanding action with the weight exerting an outward pull. Try making yourself such a device which is illustrated in the picture section. When you try it you will notice how you guide the movement entirely through a feel of what is happening with the

48

The best visual demonstration of a swinging action is the movement of a weight attached to the end of a string or handkerchief, as in the above illustration. The handkerchief, being flexible, cannot transmit power through leverage.

weight. So long as the weight is swung, the string will be taut, regardless of whether the swing is short or long.

I also have a device known as the pro swing. It is built like a regular club, except that the bottom part of the shaft is a spring to which is attached a weight comparable to the clubhead. It is a most accurate check on whether or not you are swinging properly. Whether you swing the weight on the string or the pro swing, the moment you deviate from the proper action you will notice that everything goes wrong.

I again refer you to the picture section, where you will find a picture showing me holding a club along with a handkerchief to which a knife is tied. I am executing a swing approximately through a half circle. The handkerchief serves to check on the swing of the club. If I push or pull on the shaft, though it may still move through an arc, the movement of knife on handkerchief will not coincide.

There is only one swing, the correct one. That, no matter how often you overhear golfers talk about altering or changing their swings, or hear them say they can swing in many ways—upright, flat, inside out, outside in, etc.

In golf, a swing is a positive, indivisible motion backward and forward. It has definite form or shape, which is an arc, or part of a circle.

A swing has perfect rhythm which can be put to waltz-time music. It is a measure of time, as is the pendulum of a clock. Like the pendulum, it takes the same measure of time to swing, irrespective of the length of the swing.

50

Thus, a short putt takes the same measure of time to complete as does a full drive, if the same club is used and held at the same place. The idea of swinging fast or slow is not possible in the same length of swing. Therefore, since a true swing takes the same measure of time, the longer the swing, the greater the force, or speed. The shorter the swing, the less the speed, or force.

Remember Galileo's law of falling bodies. Drop a solid, light weight and a heavy weight. Both take the same time to fall, irrespective of the difference in their weight. But the greater the weight, the more force in striking the object. So the more power you put into the swinging motion of the clubhead, the greater force you create. But if you overpower the swing, the force will die.

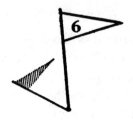

SWINGING vs. HACKING

ALTHOUGH THIS CHAPTER is entitled "Swinging vs. Hacking," it could as easily be called "Swinging vs. Hitting," or "Swinging vs. Jerking."

After listening in on countless locker-room discussions, perhaps I should have called the chapter "Swinging vs. Hitting." Remember: there is one categorical imperative in golf. HIT THE BALL. There are no minor absolutes.

Are there hitters as opposed to swingers?

You have heard golfers catalogued into groups of hitters and swingers. But such people do not know what they are talking about.

All great golfers had to learn how to hit the ball. Because of their natural start they may not realize that. But, and I emphasize this for those who call themselves hitters, they cannot get the maximum force into the clubhead unless they swing.

Press, drag, push, snap, pull, etc.: none is a swing. Bobby Jones copied the action of a wonderful swinger, Stewart Maiden, when he was a boy.

So, where great golfers are involved, you cannot say,

"Swingers vs. Hitters." They are all swingers. Where the other kind are concerned, I think the best title becomes "Swingers vs. Hackers," or "Jerkers."

The first great difference between a swinger and a hacker is that the former gains better control over the clubhead.

The swinger proves that you cannot move the clubhead faster than you can swing it. Thus, he is not guilty of the hacker's greatest failing, of trying to generate power with which to hit the ball by rushing the backswing, jerking the club from its position behind the ball, and then compounding his error by again rushing the downswing.

Were it possible to break down this noxious caricature of a golf swing, you would discover that the hacker, not knowing how to begin the swing back, tries to begin his downswing even before he has finished his upswing. This is not physically possible.

Unfortunately, in seeking instruction, the hacker frequently is told:

"Let the club do the work."

The teacher knows what he has in mind, and it is correct. But he uses the wrong words. What he means is that you cannot move the clubhead faster than you can swing it. So he should tell you to swing the clubhead. But he says: "Let the club do the work."

What sometimes happens is that the hacker transposes from one failing to another. He then tries to let the club do the work—without his participation. He does not use his hands, perhaps because he hasn't been told about the "feel" of the swing, lets the club fall against the ball. It is a fluffy stroke without any power or authority motivating the club's action.

There must be force in the swing. When the hacker learns that that force comes through controlling the clubhead with the hands and fingers, he is ready to move into the class of the swinger, where all good golfers belong.

This is a good time to distinguish between leverage and centrifugal force.

Leverage is a word which belongs on a golf course only when the greenskeeper uses a crowbar in an effort to uproot a deeply imbedded rock. In prying, he presses down hard, in order to force the object up. The power applied moves in one direction, while the object to which it is applied moves in the opposite direction.

This is what the hacker persists in attempting on the

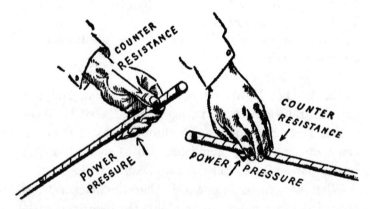

The head of a golf club can be moved in a circular path through the application of leverage, as the drawings show. Such golfers have not learned the meaning of swinging the clubhead. The result is a poor shot.

54

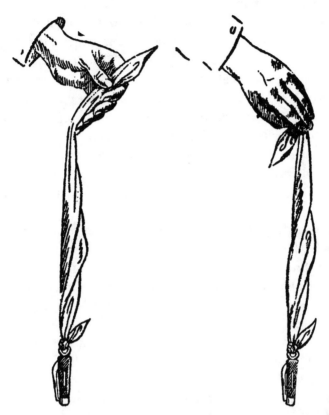

Although pressure will make a clubhead move, it cannot cause the swinging of the knife on the end of the handkerchief. That can be moved only by a swinging motion. Notice that the pressure applied in the above drawings bent the flexible handkerchief without swinging the knife.

golf course. He presses against the club with his fingers, as if to use it for levering. He creates pressure, which becomes a terrible strain on the arms. Try making a tight fist. Notice how it strains your fingers, the pain extending all the way up the arm. That is pressure.

You cannot create a swing by pressure. In a swing, everything is moving in the same direction around a center. That is centrifugal force. In the swing, you hold the club as taught in Chapter Three, and perform an action which is a joy. Thus, you can reduce to pain vs. joy the difference between exerting leverage, which is a painful process, as against swinging, which is exhilerating.

Swinging becomes an action which is definite in itself, which is subject to its own peculiar laws and which is entirely free of, and distinct from, leverage. The swing has clubhead and ball moving in the same direction. The two are diametrically opposed methods of applying power.

And yet a word of caution. When you are advised, "don't press," it does not mean avoid hitting hard. It means do not use pressure.

I shall go into more complete detail in the chapter "Obstacles to Swinging."

Now I shall attempt to explain how to acquire a swing.

HOW TO ACQUIRE A SWING

"FROM ONE LEARN ALL." From a single instance infer
the whole. This is a translation from the Latin: "Ab uno
disce omnus."

I repeat: the golf swing can be readily taught, and consistently performed only if it is conceived as one motion.

The swing gives you everything: the ability to hit the
ball properly, both for distance and direction.

In swinging you use power to create force. Power
is your strength and energy. Force is speed times weight.
Thus, the more speed in your swing, the more force-
fully will the clubhead strike the ball. You have the
POWER. You CREATE the FORCE. Therefore, only
you can use it.

Since the swing is the result of the proper use of the
hands and fingers, I must become repetitious. I said, in
Chapter Three on how to hold the club, that the overlapping grip has all the qualities and none of the defects
of the others. It also permits the two most important
fingers—the thumb and forefinger—to best do their
proper jobs.

The hands give you the FEEL of the swing. In one of my lessons, I think I expressed the thought perfectly, when I said:

"WHATEVER YOUR HANDS TAKE HOLD OF, THEY MUST HAVE CONTROL OF."

Before taking hold of the club I want you to again try this little exercise. Place your arms straight out. Bring the palms of your hands together. Study the illustrations in the picture section.

Now place the right hand on top of the left. Close your fingers as if bringing them over the shaft. Except that the small finger of the right hand is brought to rest on the forefinger of the left, you have your hands placed in the way they should hold the handle of the shaft.

Now take a club. Repeat the process. Try the feel of the club. Make sure that feel is principally through the thumb and forefinger of the two hands. Although the shaft is placed diagonally across the palm of your left hand, it is through those fingers that contact is made with the club. Remember: your thumb is your principal finger!

In being told to place the club shaft across the palm, too many pupils misunderstand, or they are not told clearly enough. They tend to grasp the club as if to pull a rope in a tug-of-war. This leaves the fingers without the feel of the clubhead. You become dead-handed because the club is grasped so tightly that the muscles of the arms are paralyzed. To understand what I mean make a tight fist and exert pressure. Notice how the pain shoots up your arm.

I said in Chapter Four, on the stance, that the square

stance is the only one which permits you to be perfectly balanced. The others are not natural stances, and you are not truly balanced when you use them.

I realize that there are great golfers using either the open or closed stances. I read recently an article in which one great golfer advised the square stance as best for beginners. I say it is best for all golfers, whether beginners or champions.

I shall concede one point. A champion can afford to take liberties. A Joe Kirkwood or Jack Redmond, famous trick shot artists, can demonstrate many amazing ways in which a golf ball can be hit.

You may not be a champion. Until you become one you cannot take liberties with your swing. And when you are a champion you will learn that you cannot fool around with your swing and remain a champion.

You cannot become a trick shot artist until you have mastered completely the proper manner in which to control a golf club to strike a ball. My purpose being to teach you to play good golf, not to perform tricks, we shall concentrate on the basic principle—the swing.

When, in 1916, I found myself with only one leg, I had no idea of the kind of golf I would be able to play. I wanted to play, and after my first round, I realized I could still play and enjoy the game, and that my ideas were true.

Playing on one leg made me realize that too many golfers tried to keep in mind far too many things. Because I was playing on one leg I had to concentrate hard on one fact, that I must swing the club to maintain my balance. As a result, I never lost my balance during that first round, nor have I at any time since. I went home to do a great deal of thinking.

I CAME TO THE CONCLUSION THAT THE PROPER SWING TAKES CARE OF ONE'S BALANCE.

Let me show you the proper swing. Here is my gadget, the pocket knife at the end of a string or handkerchief. I hold the handkerchief between thumb and forefinger and swing it. Do the same with the gadget I suggested you make. Notice that it swings only when you make the proper motion.

Jerk your hand. The object does not swing. The steady motion like that of a pendulum is the swing.

Or try this stunt. Hold a golf club with your thumb and forefinger. Swing the clubhead to and fro. Notice how easily it swings back and forth, and how evenly. The same motion, only this time with the clubhead properly in both hands, is the swing. Extend the arc of the swing and you will extend the distance the golf ball travels.

Study the drawings on page 49. You will see the same thing in the picture section. Put your gadget to work, swinging in the same manner. The proper swing makes the handkerchief draw taut because a swinging action is always an expanding action, with the weight exerting the outward pull.

In the photographs corresponding to this chapter you will notice that I am holding a club along with the knife tied to a handkerchief. As I swing through a half circle I know, from the movement of the handkerchief, whether or not I am swinging properly.

Should I push or pull on the shaft of the club, it may still appear to the unpracticed observer as if the club is travelling through the proper arc. But the handkerchief fails to move with the club, telling me immediately that I have not swung properly.

Leverage may have a result which looks similar to swinging. But pretend that the shaft on your club is rubber instead of steel. Now visualize what happens. Failure to swing would result in the rubber shaft not moving in the arc of the circle.

You MUST get the feel of the action, especially since you cannot see your own swing. It is not HOW do you feel, but WHAT do you feel. I cannot tell you HOW you see, hear, taste, smell or feel. But WHAT you use your senses for, you must be aware of.

Only an experienced eye can see the difference between the true swinging movement and the movement through leverage. The casual observer cannot. But the check of the handkerchief, or string, on a weight, when moved together with the club, is complete and convincing.

Practice constantly with the weight. Learn how to swing it together with a club. It may take a little time to master, but the result will be extremely gratifying.

When you have mastered this technique you will discover that you have learned to distinguish between swinging and levering. You will have learned the difference through sight and, vastly more important, through feel.

I am sure you will not react as did one of my pupils,

THE HANDS INITIATE THE SWING OF THE CLUBHEAD.

THROUGH THEM YOU MAINTAIN THE FEEL, SENSE CONTROL

OF WHAT IS BEING DONE FROM START TO FINISH.

The artist has deliberately omitted the body outlines in the drawings on these two pages, to prove that it is the hands which control the swing and through which you sense the

THE BODY—HIPS, SHOULDERS, HEAD—RESPONDS AUTOMATI-

CALLY TO CONSCIOUS EFFORT TO MAINTAIN CONTROL OF

CLUBHEAD (WITH THE HANDS) THROUGHOUT THE STROKE.

feel of the clubhead. The other parts of the body respond to the movement of the hands. You do not consciously move your body while wielding the club.

63

whom I questioned about whether or not she had practiced the string method. Her answer was:

"Yes, I tried it. But I don't think I got the right kind of string. It kept bending and wouldn't keep straight."

Must I repeat that the motion is that of a pendulum, that its fundamental characteristic is the same whether swung through a small arc (putting) or a large one (driving).

The maximum arc is a complete circle attained through the action of the wrists acting as hinges. If perfect, the golf stroke would be a circle. Neither the golf club nor the pendulum complete a circle; they complete part of a circle. Although no one makes an absolutely perfect swinging motion, the action is that of a pendulum. The closer you approach a perfect swing, the steadier and more consistent will be the results.

An objection raised to my explanation of a swing is that what is applicable to a weight being whirled on the end of a string may not be applicable to swinging a club which starts in one direction (backswing) and then changes direction.

In answer, think of David facing Goliath with the stone in his sling. Secondly, the pendulum changes direction, and with no difficulty. The weight swinging on the end of the string changes direction with no difficulty.

The explanation is in the wrists, which act as hinges. The unified action of the two wrists, which are flexible, permit you to expand the arc of your swing, i.e. from a putting stroke to driving. They permit you to change the direction of the path of the clubhead without hindering the true swinging motion, without disturbing the rhythmic characteristics of the swing.

Here you approach your goal, the ability to identify the correct action of the clubhead through the sense of touch, or feeling. That sense of feel is GAINED THROUGH THE PROPER USE OF THE HANDS. IT MUST BE SENSED FROM THE VERY START OF A STROKE.

If the stroke fails to START as a swinging action, it seldom develops into one. Then how do you properly start this movement?

First, forget about the other parts of your body. Yes, they move. But the action of the swing takes a fraction of time, not enough to permit you to think about "stiff left arm," "right arm close to the side," "bend the left knee," etc., etc. Your power would go from your fingers to your arms, or knees, or whatever you were thinking about. That is the paralysis by analysis which ruins your game.

The answer is much simpler. You start the proper movement through the hands. They transmit the power to what is being swung. Those hands, at the end of the shaft, initiate and guide the action. Although the two hands work as a unit you use the hand at the end, the left for the right-handed golfer, for control.

But, remember, golf is neither a right-handed nor a left-handed game. It is a two-handed game. But the one at the end of the shaft remains in control throughout. Therefore it is the controlling and directing agency. This also is true when swinging an ax or a heavy hammer which requires the use of two hands.

The sensation of what is done with the clubhead is felt in the hands, which are the medium through which conscious effort should be directed. All other physical actions of the body follow as responsive movement.

Equally as important is to start your stroke in the proper mental frame. Your greatest mental problem, as you are about to stroke, is tenseness through fear, which is the result of confusion in your mind. You fear you will forget one of the many pieces of information you think must be remembered while you stroke.

Since swinging implies a free, easy rhythm, tenseness, which virtually locks the muscles in your body, is an insurmountable barrier to swinging.

To overcome tenseness try holding the club between your thumb and forefinger, as I explained the method a few pages back. As you walk along the golf course swing the club back and forth, gradually increasing the arc as much as your two fingers will permit. As you get the feel of the swinging movement of the clubhead your tenseness will disappear.

Repeat the process, this time with the club properly held in both hands. Swing it back and forth. When the feel is right notice how your body moves easily in response to the action of the hands. You will enjoy complete freedom from tenseness. No part of your body will set up a resistance to the natural physical response by the body, to the swinging action.

That, and holding the golf club and weighted-string simultaneously, are the best suggestions I can give to help you learn to know and identify the swing by feel. And learning by feel is the only way to learn the swing so that you will make steady and permanent progress as a golfer. No one else, not even the finest teacher in the world, can learn to know for you the feel of the swing. Only you can have that, just as only you can do your own walking.

A word or two about the waggle, which is a very important part of your golf game. If properly applied the waggle will help you to develop the proper feel of the swing.

It should not be performed aimlessly. When waggling before taking your shot you should make a conscious application of power through your hands and fingers. Move the clubhead back and forth. When done with the club held correctly and while standing in the proper manner, the waggle will help you gain the feel of the club. It will give you an increasing command over its action.

When you have mastered the waggle you will find it easy to extend that to the full swing. Make the swing, backward and forward. It is an excellent physical drill. It will give you balance, feel and control over the clubhead. Practiced conscientiously, the waggle will give you the freedom and certainty of movement, as well as the habit of mental concentration which golf demands.

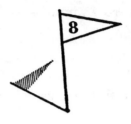

TIMING AND RHYTHM

WHEN YOU STROKE with timing and rhythm, there is no feeling of physical effort or visible evidence of the application of power. That's why cardiacs can play golf when all other sports may be forbidden them.

When you stroke with timing and rhythm, the ball sails straight down the fairway, and for distance. IT IS EFFORTLESS POWER, NOT POWERFUL EFFORT. The fact that you can hit a ball a great distance without physical exertion is hard for some people to understand. The tyro sees the expert get great distance and he concludes that he can match that effort only by straining and tugging in an effort to hit the ball a tremendous wallop. I hardly need describe the almost certain result: a trickling ball which skips in rabbit hops for a few yards.

I am convinced that most players never actually felt the sensation of striking the ball with a true swing. That's why they strain and tug so furiously, convert into such hard physical labor a game which should never be more than a pleasurable pastime.

Fine timing and rhythm are the products of correct

swinging. As I said in Chapter Five, the swing has perfect rhythm which can be put to waltz-time music.

There are critics who insist that everyone knows you have to swing the clubhead, but that you must do much more than swing, if you wish to play good golf. I disagree. You need only learn to swing the clubhead so that it will strike the ball the most forceful and most accurate blow possible with the power at your command. The rest will take care of itself.

You create maximum force by developing clubhead speed in swinging. But you cannot force a swing. Unfortunately, too many people think they can force the power with which they strike the clubhead against the ball. That is not so. A swing is a definite motion. You, to get maximum force, must get all the power you can into that motion, but without disturbing it, without forcing it from the arc of the swing. You must swing with authority.

Perfect swinging is perfect rhythm. I shall repeat that over and over again. A stroke to make the ball travel a few inches, takes the same measure of time as one to make it go 200 yards, if the same club is used.

A pupil recently described his sensation after watching Sam Snead play a round of golf. He was perplexed, because watching had failed to give him a single pointer which could help his own game.

The pupil was paying Snead a high compliment. He is one of the most beautiful swingers the game ever developed. Snead gets tremendous speed into the clubhead, the result of the steady, smooth application of power through swinging. There is no waste of power, no counteraction which produces contortions that might be mistakenly identified as the keynote of success in the stroke.

Had my pupil watched Snead correctly he would have learned something. He should have watched the action of Snead's hands when going through the swinging motion. If you have the opportunity, watch those hands. Watch the clubhead. Notice the smooth rhythm with which it picks up speed from the moment it is started back until the ball has been struck.

A characteristic of centrifugal application of power— i.e. swinging—is its apparent effortlessness. There is no strain, as in levering. A giant wheel spun at the rate of 1,000 or 2,000 revolutions per minute, gives no hint of the terrific power driving it because it is applied evenly and smoothly.

But if there is a flaw in the construction of the wheel, it will fly apart under the force developed. Parts will be thrown a great distance, with much damage resulting. The power driving a perfectly functioning wheel is ever present, but the rhythm of its application does not readily suggest force, as measured by the results obtained.

It is the same in golf. The smoother and more rhythmic the swing, the less you are likely to suspect the range of the power, when watching its application by an expert.

The idea, I fear, is so simple that even fine golfers hesitate to accept it. One well-known golfer came to my indoor school for instruction last Winter. I told him there could not be much wrong with his game. I added:

"The trouble with you good players is that you are always trying to learn why you hit a shot badly, instead of trying to understand what it is you do when you hit one well."

Then he made the most amazing confession. He said: "To tell you the truth, sometimes when I am playing well it seems so easy it is actually disappointing."

That is the point exactly. He could not appreciate that freedom of timing and rhythm are recognizable, so he got the idea something was wrong and was disappointed. That, although he was playing perhaps the best golf of his career.

He worried over what he did wrong on an occasional bad shot, as must happen to all golfers because they are human beings and not machines and thus must occasionally stray from the sense of timing and rhythm. So he did not know what to do when his game began to go bad.

ONCE YOU LEARN TO SENSE THE FEEL OF TIMING AND RHYTHM EMBODIED IN A REAL SWING, YOU WILL ALWAYS HAVE A DEFINITE PRINCIPLE WITH WHICH TO CHECK.

Without that you must forever go on groping in the dark.

I recall a magazine cartoon showing a lady golfer in a trap. She had completed her swing, and the cartoon showed the ball resting on the lip of the cup. The caption read:

"I wonder what I did right?"

That was intended as a joke conceived from the "I wonder what I did wrong," which is heard so often on the golf course. But it should be the credo of every good golfer. Every duffer should strive for the day when he can say: "I know what I did right."

No one is more surprised than the duffer when, after countless rounds of grunting and groaning, he accidentally strikes the ball with a real swing. That usually happens when he tries to play short of a hazard. Because he doesn't want distance he strikes the ball somewhat lazily and with little conscious effort. Instead of falling short, the ball will travel a great distance and even, ironically, land plump into the hazard.

In the absence of the urge to "kill" the ball, the duffer swung with timing and rhythm, with an easy movement of the club and an absence of the conflicting movements which otherwise impeded his swing.

But I must once again caution you. Do not construe from the above that the clubhead swings itself. YOU must initiate the power that swings the clubhead, with a swinging motion and with the feel of what you are doing through your hands. The carpenter uses a saw with which to cut wood, but he does not let the saw cut the wood while he stands idly watching. He uses his hands to MAKE the saw do its job.

To contrast golf with baseball, the swinging action can be developed to fullest advantage in producing both speed and precision because the ball is stationary. Hence no quick change of position has to be made in order to get into striking position, as in baseball. In golf it is just swinging.

I have often thought of Joe DiMaggio since the 1951 World Series. He lost his batting timing and had a great deal of difficulty until Lefty O'Doul, a former great hitter and manager, helped correct his timing.

I thought of DiMaggio because I remember reading about a year before that he had become very fond of golf and that his great ambition was to break 100. Anyone with his natural ability should have done that easily after playing only a month. I have the impression that he had the wrong idea of how to swing a golf club, that he was trying to swing with his body instead of his hands. Only thus can a true swing, with proper rhythm and timing, be gained.

Your own swing, if it is real, will be truly rhythmic, with the timing felt in the motion of the clubhead.

So swing it!

WOODS, IRONS AND THE PUTTER

"I AM COMPLETELY unaware of making any attempt to swing one club differently than another."

The above is taken out of context from Byron Nelson's remark, which was quoted in full in the first chapter.

Nelson, one of the great masters of golf, is telling you that the stroke, in its basic essentials, is the same with all clubs.

This is my reason for avoiding detailed discussions on how to use the individual clubs: "How to Drive," "How to Play the Different Irons," "How to Play Woods from the Fairway," "How to Pitch," "How to Putt," etc.

For many reasons, a few of which I shall explain and many more of which you will learn from experience, you will at times have to vary the swing.

BUT YOU MUST NEVER VARY FROM THE SWING.

No matter what club you use, from driver down to the putter, it is always a swing. Nelson went on to explain that the difference between clubs took care of the different requirements of the shot.

Golf's development has been greatest in the making of

clubs, the many types of which are familiar even to the duffer. They have made golf so much easier that the United States Golf Association virtually rebuilt Oakland Hills to toughen it for the 1951 Open championship. Since almost all other courses haven't been changed in years, except to make them easier by cutting the rough, the development of clubs has resulted in some phenominal scoring. The livelier golf balls have also played their part.

Notice, in the picture section corresponding to this chapter, that clubs matched in sets are built so that those needed for greater distances have longer shafts. Thus you automatically stand further back for a drive than for a shorter-shafted iron shot. As for the putter, its shaft permits you to virtually stand over the ball when swinging.

There is, however, the one common denominator with every club; to hit the ball properly you must SWING THE CLUBHEAD.

The length of the shaft, the lie of the clubhead, and the distance you stand from the ball determine the plane in which the club is swung. Thus swinging with a five iron (mashie) is more upright than with the driver. But there is no variation in the nature of the swing. The variation comes in the angle in which the club is held.

What makes it difficult for some to understand this is that no two players swing exactly alike. Although the swing is perfect motion there are as many variations in the manner of swinging as there are players. All try to swing. But draw several circles freehand. You'll discover that no two will be alike.

75

You will be told that Byron Nelson takes a three-quarters swing. If you observed Nelson and Ben Hogan you would see a great difference, mainly in the way the clubhead is moved. Nelson lifts the club back. Hogan swings it back. But both of these great golfers do the same thing in the forward motion on every shot. When they hit the ball, they swing.

All good golfers, however, can and do vary their own swings to meet individual problems they face. Many years ago, I saw Walter Hagen hit out of a trap while standing practically on one leg because the ball was caught on the side of a steep embankment. What is more, he chipped into the cup for a birdie.

If conditions require the ball to rise abruptly, the player uses a club with considerable loft. But he swings. The change is only the plane in which the swing occurs.

Playing from difficult lies involves special problems in adapting the swing to such conditions. When faced with uphill or downhill lies, or sidehill lies up or down, you must make allowances in order to maintain your balance while stroking.

When you walk uphill or downhill, or along the side of a hill, do you give any thought to the adjustments you make to keep your balance? Of course not. Your muscular actions respond to the job of keeping the body balanced, without your conscious effort. So it will be in playing the golf stroke, once you have acquired the knack of swinging until it is a habit.

When faced with uphill or downhill lies you should take a stance which places you in the same position in relation to the ball as you would be were you stroking

on level ground. YOU LET YOURSELF LEAN TO
THE TERRAIN. Playing uphill, lean backwards; playing downhill, lean forward. Thus, you maintain an even
balance.

One of the popular fallacies in golf is that the irons
require more of a hit than do the woods. Conceded
that, when watching the experts, you sense that they
may "punch" with irons, which is not apparent in the
fuller stroke with wood clubs. But remember, you cannot move any clubhead faster than you can swing it.

I must remind you of the distinction made between
hitting and swinging earlier in these pages. I also said
that no one swings perfectly. And all golfers, at times,
are struck with the impulse to use more power than can
be applied properly by swinging.

When injecting that additional power which is beyond
control, the golfer introduces leverage, which we mentioned earlier. If introduced from the start, leverage is
disastrous. When it creeps in just before impact, it does
very little noticeable damage, provided the stroke has
started as a swing and has remained one almost to the
instant of impact.

Introduced a fraction before impact, that leverage is
restricted to hand and wrist action. It does not involve
conflicting actions between body movement and arm
movement, the natural consequences of the introduction
of leverage at the start of the stroke.

If leverage is applied at the start of the stroke it can
never develop into a swing. But if the action starts as
a swing, the hands and arms will swing on through,
maintaining the swinging characteristic even though

some small degree of leverage develops through the hands and wrist just before impact. You had best forget about leverage. It is not the right kind of force. Leave it out of your vocabulary.

Iron shots also appear to be "hit" or "punched" because, being shorter strokes, they require less than a full swing and thus do not need the full body turn necessary for wood clubs. The shorter the shot, however, the greater is the impulse to press or jerk the club.

On short shots the bending or flexing of the wrists is just as necessary, IN A RESPONSIVE SENSE. The weight of the club pulls the arms to where the wrists bend, just before the change in direction takes place.

Always bear in mind that the wrists act as hinges which join the hands and arms. Thus, the natural outward pull of the clubhead will cause them to bend as the speed of the clubhead builds up to its maximum at impact. This is truest of the real swinging action, and it is independent of any conscious effort to put "wrist snap" into the stroke. The wrists are responsive to motion. They never initiate the swinging action.

When the clubhead is changing direction, the hand action brings about a position of the wrists, in relation to the forearms, quite different from their position in addressing the ball. When the clubhead returns to the position of impact, the same as that in the address, the hands must also return to their original position. Otherwise, the face of the club could not be brought squarely against the ball. This return to original position is brought about by the swinging action, without any conscious effort to put so-called "wrist snap" into the stroke.

Trying to gain distance by conscious introduction of wrist action introduces leverage through too powerful action of the right hand. It results in a shot which usually goes far off line to the left. Never forget that, since the left hand (in a right-handed golfer) is the one at the end of the shaft, that left hand must not be overpowered.

Conscious use of wrist action is most common to those who failed to learn a swinging action with the clubhead. Their effort results in the forward sweep of the hands being practically stopped by the time the clubhead reaches the ball. All that is left is a forward flick of the wrists.

The wrists are, when used properly, of vast importance. They make it possible, as already explained, to retain the easy, smooth rhythm of a swinging action through the change in direction of the clubhead from the back sweep until it has made contact and followed through. The hinges on a door do not make it a swinging door. But they allow it to become one. Thus with the wrists. Their action, like the rest of the body, must be entirely responsive to the main purpose of making the clubhead move with a swinging action, through the medium of the hands.

Your eye has deceived you if, in watching others, you think that the stroke with the iron club is more like a hit than the stroke with the wood. With the iron, as with the wood, you use the same guide to controlled speed; you swing the clubhead. With the irons, as with the woods, you must develop that sense of feel of what is happening with the clubhead.

Naturally, as already explained, you must vary the swing from long strokes to short ones. That is because the action is cut down. Visualize the difference in the arc of the swing with the driver and the putter. Yet both are swings, and there is no variation in the character of their action. You swing, from the tee shot right down to the putt.

Beginners—all golfers, for that matter—unfortunately have more difficulty maintaining the swing in the shorter strokes than in the longer ones. This is just as true of good players, who make more bad shots on the short ones than from the tee. You will have that trouble until you have become impregnated with the idea of sensing the feel of the clubhead at all times. And how is that done? Through the hands, of course.

In the short stroke there is less motion in which to acquire the feel of the clubhead. Since the longer action of the full stroke gives you more awareness you should always play better off the tee. There also is a tendency, on the short stroke, to hurry the thing through and have done with it. That always results in leverage. A hurried start has no place in a swing, which always should begin slowly and smoothly. It is timed force that counts.

As for the putt, it is the payoff stroke on each hole. You can recover from a bad tee shot, but never from a missed putt. A long putt will cut at least a stroke from your score.

Bobby Locke and Jim Ferrier built great reputations as putters. You hear less about Ben Hogan's putting, but he also is outstanding. A subpar round always requires excellent putting. That's why it has been the subject of more detailed study and discussion than any other phase of golf. That's why there are so many strangely designed putters, some of which were barred from tournaments. All this in an effort to help the golfer in his vain quest for an easy solution to putting. The closer the hole, the more tricks are tried to get it in.

The solution IS easy, and you can find it with a normal putter. Just swing. The stroke with the putter differs in none of its essentials from the stroke with any other club. You just swing the clubhead.

Obviously, the arc of the putting swing is much shorter than the arc in swinging with the driver. But it is a swing. And because there is so much less of a problem in maintaining balance throughout the stroke, putting should be easier than other parts of golf. There is so much less power to be applied in putting that there is correspondingly less need for responsive body action. (See illustrations).

Naturally, in putting, as in any stroke, you must follow the fundamentals of holding the club, taking the proper position to play the stroke. You must move the clubhead with a pendulum-like motion.

In the grip, although many good players use the reverse overlap, I cannot see any reason to alter the way of holding the club to obtain better control. Bobby Locke is good with his natural overlap.

If you swing properly, proficient putting then becomes a matter of practice. The swing and practice will give you the sense of touch which subconsciously makes you strike the ball with the exact force needed to reach the cup. Practice and experience will help you learn the contour of the putting surface. It will teach you judgment in determining direction to compensate for the roll of the green between the ball and the cup.

True, there are a great many putting techniques in use today. Many of them are awkward, but some appear to be effective. But I insist that a simplified, direct method of learning to swing the clubhead is the safest approach to acquiring consistent skill on the putting green.

Here I must warn you against the temptation to strike the pose you think resembles that of a player you admire. If you think in terms of the pose, your mind is concentrated on body posture and not on the vitally important subject of hand action.

Pay more attention to POISE than to POSE. I am reminded of a pupil who developed a most perfect style. But she did not hit the ball well. When I took hold of her hand to swing the clubhead, she said:

"I wish I could feel it that way."

Surprised, I said:

"Well, why don't you do that."

"You see," she answered, "I am an actress. I can act the part, but I cannot feel it."

And, as she herself explained, if you cannot feel the part, you cannot be good.

Once you understand what swinging means and know how to identify it through feel, you can swing a club from almost any position. Trick shot artists prove this. A picture in the photographic section shows me hitting the ball while sitting in a chair. I have driven many balls more than 200 yards sitting thus. I use this simple device to prove to pupils that, whereas there is one simple and comfortable way to stand to the ball, the square stance, there are many ways that one can stand and still swing.

Learn to swing: that is the important thing, whether you use a wood, iron or putter. Learn to recognize when you are swinging and when you are not swinging. Then you will develop your own pattern of swinging just as you have developed that of walking. When you have advanced that far, you may vary your swing from time to time, consciously, or even subconsciously.

The ability to swing, and to know a swinging action by feel, is the only hope for permanent improvement in golf. With that knowledge will come, almost automatically, the knowledge of variations in the various clubs, of which there are 14 in the full bag.

OBSTACLES TO SWINGING

THE OBSTACLES to swinging are many, so many that I shall summarize the major ones first, before going into detail.

An entry in the obstacle derby consists of misplaced ambition and fear about which I shall go into detail in the next chapter. By this time you should be aware that leverage is an obstacle to swinging.

There are others, such as:

Not having a positive understanding of WHAT should be swung. (The clubhead, of course.)

Not having a positive understanding of the MEDIUM with which the clubhead is swung. (The hands and fingers, and primarily the fingers.)

Not having a definite knowledge of what is initiative action and what is responsive motion. (Cause and effect, with the latter capable of being seen and photographed. The cause is recognized entirely through the sense of feel. The feel cannot be photographed. Have you ever seen a picture of an ache or a pain? You have, however, seen pictures which depict pain, which is the result of the feeling, not the feeling itself.)

The greatest obstacle is pressure, in any form. "Don't press" does not mean avoid trying to hit hard. It means do not use pressure (leverage), for then you will not be able to move the clubhead as fast as your power is capable of. Use your power through the medium of the hands and fingers to swing the clubhead, not through your arms to keep them straight, or through your wrists to make them cock. Nor do you have to brace yourself against the force of the swing.

Remember, centrifugal force means receding from a center. That center is ZERO. The larger the circumference of the arc the greater the force. Somewhere in your body the SWING will find a center. But you cannot swing with zero. You swing with the hands.

Here I wish to discuss head lifting. Contrary to widespread belief, head lifting invariably is an EFFECT of bad swinging, not the CAUSE. It is not the disease, but the symptom of the disease, just as fever is a symptom, rather than the ailment itself. Remember, there is a blind man's golf championship.

There is but one real cure for head lifting, and that is to learn how to swing, to learn the proper hand and finger control which produces the swing. Unfortunately, too many golfers consider head lifting the disease itself. How often have you muffed a shot, and your partner will shake his head and say:

"You peeked."

His tone implies that the cure is simple. Just keep your head down. He is partially correct. The cure is simple. Resort to swinging, first making sure that you are in a balanced stance, and you will no longer lift

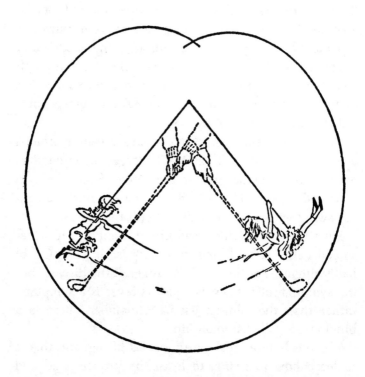

A child swinging in a swing exactly parallels the action of swinging a clubhead with the hands. The child, just as do the hands, starts to swing slowly. In both there is a gradual and smooth increase in the application of speed to develop force to swing swiftly, in the case of the child, and to hit the ball for distance, in the case of the golfer.

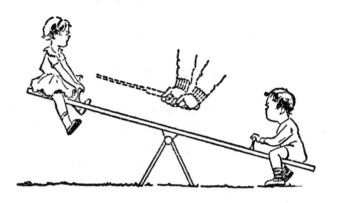

In contrast to the swinging child, the seesaw is a visual example of the principle of leverage. Both ends, on which the children sit, apply power by moving in opposite directions. Notice that the same method of applying power to the golf clubhead will "break" the wrists and result in a quick and jerky application of power.

your head. When you swing, you are placing first things first. Head lifting is caused by fear and anxiety. You are seeking the result before you have struck the ball. You did not trust your swing.

Why are so many golfers guilty of leverage?

There are several answers. First, there is the overwhelming ambition to use more power than the swing can take. The word "hit" frequently inspires that urge, which is the reason for my leaning to the word "strike." When that happens, the golfer braces himself and levers instead of swings in an effort to kill the ball.

Shall we study "hitting" in the light of its definition? The dictionary defines "hitting" as "bringing into VIOLENT contact." "Striking" on the other hand is defined as "touching with some force," or "giving a blow to." The rules of golf say that the ball must be fairly STRUCK, not pushed, scraped or spooned.

Leonardo da Vinci, the famous Renaissance artist, described a blow as "the son of motion, the grandson of force, whilst their mutual ancestor is weight."

What do we discover? Violence is meant when using the word "hit." Violence suggests suddenness of action. Violence is out of place when one is holding a golf club in his hands.

Thus, "strike" is the correct word. The great difference between "hitting" and "striking" is not in the amount of power applied but in the manner of its application.

The manner of application is the difference between swinging and levering, the difference between a sudden, hurried attempt to exert power and a smooth, rhythmic

88

one. Levering is painful and poor hitting. It is like using a club to pry a stone out of the ground. Swinging is striking.

You can hit the ball by employing leverage. But you can strike the ball faster with a swinging action than you can through any other means. And by swinging you still retain proper control over your effort.

The principle of centrifugal force assures this. Do you question it? Then back to our Webster. If I fail in my quest to improve your golf, I shall, at least, succeed in improving your vocabulary. Webster says that centrifugal force, which recedes from the center, is a force directed outward when a body is made to move in a curved path. The body, in this case, is the club.

It is difficult for many to appreciate that centrifugal force, i.e. swinging, will produce greater distance and better control. It is not consistent with past experiences in other sports, where the natural instinct was to turn on the power all at once.

A swinging action must begin smoothly and rhythmically. The force producing it must be applied gradually. At no time during the swing can there be a quick, jerky movement. That destroys the swinging action. Therefore, steadiness, not speed, is the keynote in beginning the application of power in the swing. Speed is developed later.

When beginning the stroke hypnotized by the determination to "hit" the ball, you subconsciously try to make a quick application of your power. It is made at some intermediate point between the source, the hands, the center of gravity of the body, and the finish, the clubhead.

Such attempts fail because they are impossible to achieve. It is like attempting to increase the speed of a weight swinging at the end of a string held in one hand, by pressing on the string with the other. Leverage is the only result of such action and leverage always finds the two ends of the medium moving in opposite directions.

There are many visible results of such actions. One is the sight of the golfer pulling his left foot back from its normal position as he strokes. His weight, most of it, is supported on the right leg at the finish of the stroke, leaving him off balance. CENTRIFUGAL FORCE CREATES AND GOVERNS BALANCE.

The hurried, jerky start is another. However, you must do more than start the club easily and deliberately on its backswing. That may cut down the damage, but it brings little improvement if you still are contending against conflicting forces. Leverage is leverage, whether the slow prying of a heavy object with a strong iron bar or the faster wielding of a golf club.

In short, a swing is a swing, whether it is long or short. It always has its own peculiar distinguishing characteristics. These are the power applied through the point of contact with the club at the center, with the object swung always exerting an outward pull. Any one who has learned to identify the swing through the sense of feel can recognize this.

SO LONG AS YOU KNOW FROM THE SENSATION RELAYED THROUGH FEEL WITH THE

HANDS THAT YOU ARE MAINTAINING A REAL
SWINGING ACTION WITH THE CLUBHEAD, YOU
ARE FREE TO SWING AS FAST AS YOU CAN.

Some people may be handicapped by the lack of a
sense of rhythm. Rhythm is fundamental to the swinging movement; hence it is harder for those without that
sense to learn the swing. Anyone who can walk to music
has a sense of rhythm.

I think that women may be quicker than men in sensing the action of swinging the golf club. The men think
more in terms of strength and power. I refer to those
who take up golf after having played almost every game
EXCEPT golf since early childhood. In many of those
games leverage could be the means of applying power.

When I was a boy in Great Britain we played cricket.
American youngsters play baseball. I have noticed that
oarsmen noticeably find it hard to learn the swinging stroke. I mean people who have lived near water
all their lives and rowed when they were children. Law-
yers and oarsmen are typical extremes. One uses too
much brains; the other too much brawn.

Imitating consciously the style of another golfer is a
handicap. The mimic tends to confuse form with style.
Good form always improves style. Style can ruin form.

In imitation, too frequently that which is copied are
mannerisms only incidental to good golf. They certainly bear no relationship to the fundamentals of the
swing.

But the mannerisms are the ones picked up and sometimes explained in great detail in so-called instructive
treatises on golf.

91

Even should you identify and interpret correctly the movements of one or more parts of the body which are essential in swinging the club, you still have little, if any, chance of using this observation to improve your game. When you attempt this, you fail to realize that this outward appearance is only incidental to the important business of swinging the clubhead. No matter how the golfer looks, the vital thing in the stroke is that important business of SWINGING THE CLUBHEAD.

Your model in imitation did not learn that way. He did not give conscious thought to the many details in which the anatomy is involved. Also remember that you are watching him AFTER he became an expert. You forget HOW he became expert.

A great runner or clever dancer in action does not at all resemble the infant who laid the foundation for this superb skill through placing one foot before another in the laborious process of acquiring the feeling of balance.

Once you are old enough to analyze actions in terms of different movements, avoid conscious imitation of other golfers. What Sir Walter Simpson said in 1887 is still true today:

"For you or me to model ourselves on a champion is about as profitless as to copy Hamlet in the hope of becoming a Shakespeare."

True, there are many players whose style resembles that of older players who came under their observation while they were learning. But they did not consciously copy the other's style. Youngsters learn to golf with great ease by SUBCONSCIOUSLY imitating good players. Notice the emphasis on the word, subsconscious.

92

That's how Bobby Jones imitated Stewart Maiden's form when he was a youngster.

You, the adult, may no longer have the benefit of imitative instinct, which is the prize possession of young animals. The price we all pay for our increasing capacity to reason things out is the blunting of our imitative instinct.

The child watches a performance, and his mind registers a picture of the action as a whole. Then his imitative instinct lets him reproduce the action as a whole. Study once again, the pictures of the five-year-old child, Diana.

The child can imitate easily because she reduces to its fundamental that which is the swing. She does not copy the tricks of the golfer's personality. She copies that which is fundamental to all good golfers, the swing.

Thus, when Bobby Jones appeared in his first United States amateur championship at the age of fourteen, a well-known golf writer remarked, after watching him tee off from some distance away:

"I can almost believe that is Stewart Maiden hitting the ball."

Stewart Maiden was a famous golfer in his day. He was the instructor at the club in Atlanta, Ga., where Jones began his golf. I was quite familiar with his swing. Jones, incidentally, was an excellent mimic as a small boy. He used to amuse friends of the family with imitations of the peculiarities of various eccentric golfers at the club.

Boys naturally pattern their efforts on the better players they see. Since the better players are swingers, they

93

become swingers. This swinging action becomes, in time, habitual with no conscious effort involved.

Such imitativeness bears no relation to the adult's conscious effort to copy this or that detail of the action of a better golfer. He has only picked up a few highlights, where the youngster has absorbed the whole swing.

To appreciate the contrast, recall the remarkably easy rhythm often observed when a young caddie sneaks a swing with one of your clubs.

It is enough to learn to swing simply by sensing the action through feeling what is being done with the clubhead. Do not complicate matters by trying to imitate the appearance of other golfers at the same time.

Your walking gait may not be poetry in motion. But it gets results. Not everyone is a fine stylist. But everyone can develop form in doing a thing if they use intelligent methods. By form, I mean the capacity to do a thing many times over in substantially the same way. A swinging action is the surest and safest approach to acquiring dependable form in striking a golf ball.

And all good form has a swing. Swing and sway with Sammy Kaye, but don't try to sway and swing. Substitute true balance for sway. Balance is the result, the effect, the response to the imitative action of swinging the clubhead.

MENTAL HAZARDS

Now I want to discuss the greatest obstacle to learning the swing. It is the mind.

It is the mind which interferes with the business of swinging a golf club by intruding so many extraneous factors which do nothing but interfere with the swing.

You must blank from your mind all thought and concentrate upon Sir Walter Simpson's classic saying which has been quoted several times and will be quoted once again:

"There is only one categorical imperative in golf: hit the ball. There are no minor absolutes."

Daryn Hammond, in his book from which I also have quoted, said:

"Let the reader visualize clearly a swing in which the motive power is applied by and through the hands and particularly the fingers; let him cease to care what other physical processes are involved; and let him rest assured that if his brain prompts the hands and fingers to do their work, the other members of the body will probably do theirs. If he does this, he will be well on the way to achieving that crisp, decisive method of hitting a golf ball which makes the professional's game the despair of the ordinary amateur golfer."

The conscious mind always interferes with the subconscious. You may recall Helen Hicks' saying, in explanation of her losing to Virginia Van Wie in the 1933 women's championship:

"Virginia thought only about swinging, while I thought of everything—hit this way and that, place the ball, direction. And she beat me for the championship."

You, of course, know the mental side of golf which is psychological. Need I remind you of the many stories about the victories recorded by the great Walter Hagen, victories he earned by psychologically inducing his opponents to think too much.

All golfers who play in friendly matches are the victims of, or perpetrators of what has been called "How to win without cheating." This is the subtle use of psychology in a match.

You may enjoy the result of an unusually fine tee shot. Immediately your opponent will say:

"Great shot. Great shot. Tell me, exactly how did you grip your club?"

You show him your grip. He shakes his head and says:

"Funny, I thought you had your hands turned more."

If you fall into the trap, before you know it you are spraying the landscape because you have started thinking about where your hands should, or should not, be.

The mental side of golf with which we are most concerned also has you thinking too much. Too many golfers are fine until they think. As Walter Hagen replied,

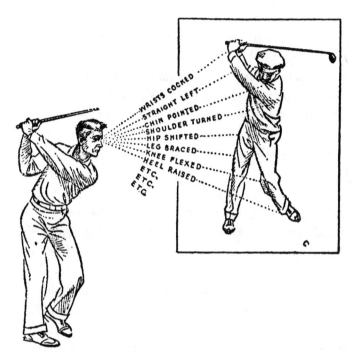

It is physically impossible, while in the process of swinging, to consciously think of the many details of the swing. Trying to remember what you saw when someone else did the swinging must interfere with what should be your subconscious control of the swing. You should think only of sensing the feel of what you are doing with the clubhead through the action of your hands.

when someone said to him that "you have to be dumb to play that game":

"You don't have to be, but it helps."

Thinking is an obstacle which strikes duffer and expert alike. When Bobby Jones came out of retirement to play in the famous master's tournament at his home club, Augusta, he played four brilliant practice rounds before the tournament, scoring 15 strokes under par for the 72 holes. Yet this man who was, perhaps, the most beautiful swinger the game ever knew, covered those same 72 holes in 10 over par in the tournament itself.

Jones' brilliant practice rounds proved that he still had the great game which made him the world's only grand slam champion. Then why the difference of 25 strokes? The mind; it interfered with his stroking when the shots counted.

Craig Wood, the former National Open champion, had trouble hitting with his driver some years ago. He resorted to teeing off with his brassie. Not expecting to outdrive his foes, Wood cleared from his mind that bogie image of "murdering" the ball. He began hitting better than ever before and won three out of the next four tournaments. Wood also won the 1941 U. S. Open championship while playing with a bad back. The back prevented him from forcing, with his hips, more power into the swing than it could carry. So he hit straighter and better than ever.

There is countless evidence about the mind spoiling the swing. A most recent case was Lew Worsham's victory over Sam Snead for the 1947 U. S. Open championship. The mind was the margin of difference. On the 18th hole of the final round Worsham overdrove the green in two. Snead was on the green. Worsham chipped back to within 29 inches of the cup. Snead's approach putt stopped 30 inches short. I can give the exact measurements because a tape was used to determine which one was furthest from the cup.

Snead stepped up to hole out, assuming that he was further away. Worsham stopped him, insisting that he thought he was further away. That's when the measurement was made which proved that Snead was away.

I happened to be sitting at the edge of the green directly behind Snead as he proceeded to make this simple putt. He stabbed at the ball, instead of swinging, and the ball rolled sharply to the right, missing the cup by at least three inches. Worsham holed out to square the match, forcing a playoff which he won. Snead, obviously, was sufficiently upset to hit, instead of swing, at the ball.

The mental image of "murdering" the ball strikes the duffer most often, but at one time or another all golfers are affected by it. The golfer whose bad mental picture makes him slash wildly at the ball does not understand that swinging a golf club for the purpose of striking a ball is a matter of using power to produce speed. When you have a golf club in your hands you are not trying to break a rock with a stone-breaker's hammer. Nor are you decapitating daisy-heads with your club, as you walk down the fairway.

The hacker's trouble is that he places much too much

emphasis upon power and not enough upon speed. Maximum speed is reached through the feel or touch, which comes only through the hands and fingers. Permit me to again quote from Daryn Hammond's book:

"The fingers bear to the other members of the body involved in the golf swing a somewhat similar relationship to that which subsists between the toes and the other members of the body involved in walking. If one walks thinking only of the action of the hips, one will instinctively take long strikes, but with little 'life.' If in walking one thinks only of the action of the knees, the effect produced will be one of feebleness and ineffectiveness.

"If, however, one walks concentrating on the action of the toes and the ankles, the stride will be short and quick, and great flexibility and vitality will be felt and suggested. The reader is invited to make the experiment and enjoy the sensation of the toes gripping the ground and promoting a rapid forward movement of the legs. The type of gait, it will be observed, is the outcome of the mental picture. It is so with golf.

"The golfer should fix it firmly in his mind that his object is not to pit his strength against the inertia of the golf ball, but to lash a responsive ball away by swinging the clubhead at it at the highest possible speed."

Speed, in short, is everything. And to attain that speed your mind must carry a clear picture of setting the clubhead in motion with your hands and fingers, and KEEPING IT IN A SWINGING MOTION AT ALL TIMES.

100

I again stress that the golf stroke IS A SINGLE, COM-PLETE ACTION. It is not a series of successive movements by different parts of the body, to be learned part by part and then pieced together into one whole. You must THINK of the stroke as a single action. In throwing a ball, for example, you give no thought to drawing back your arm and then thrusting it forward. You simply take the ball in your hand and throw it with a swinging motion.

How much thought do you give to signing your name? You can write while talking to people and each signature will be essentially the same as every other. But try consciously copying a second signature under one written naturally. The natural signature will be the easier and smoother one. The free and easy golf swing also produces the best results, and that comes only when you remove from your mind those cluttering details which make for PARALYSIS BY ANALYSIS.

In short, good golf must be played largely through subconscious control. Through constant repetition—practice—you must develop a muscular routine which makes correct stroking habitual. Then it is subconsciously controlled, and you repeat the effort whenever necessary, without giving conscious thought to how it is done.

Conscious effort to control the movement of the clubhead handicaps the expert as well as the duffer. When an expert permits his mind to interfere with his golf, it is said that he didn't concentrate.

The word concentration is, perhaps, the most misused in golf. The general meaning given it is to actively think

101

of the many details of the stroke, or perhaps one of the details. Actually, it means the opposite, the REFUSAL to allow any single detail to absorb your attention.

Miss Mary K. Brown, a former pupil of mine, was a finalist in her first women's championship in 1924. She had become famous as a tennis champion and was now playing golf. She said of her difficulties in that final:

"I think I was concentrating on concentrating, instead of on what I had in my previous matches, swinging the clubhead with my hands and watching the ball being struck."

Too many golfers think they are concentrating on the stroke when they are worrying over one detail, or, even worse, worrying over the probable outcome of the stroke. Then the muscular system tightens up, and taut muscles make it physically impossible to swing correctly.

Imagination, which has brought success to thousands of enterprising people, is a serious mental hazard in golf, especially to beginners. How much easier it would be to teach, to learn, and to swing, if we could but turn off our imaginations as we do a faucet, the moment we step onto the golf course. Stop thinking and become aware of feeling what you are doing. What thinking you do should be with your hands and fingers.

The imagination makes the beginner, blithely unaware of the inconsistency of his action, detail to the teacher his theory of what is wrong with his game. As Sir Walter Simpson said in 1887, one must stand for theorizing by a player as a concession to him as a thinking animal. But the player must recognize his theorizing as a recreation and appreciate that it can become a serious obstacle to his progress.

The golfer theorizes because he fails to appreciate that you learn the game through sense of touch, or feel. Too many think you learn through the sense of sight. When you depend upon sight instead of concentrating upon the fundamental of learning the method of stroking, you try to reproduce certain physical actions seen in others.

Then it is that you can be sidetracked in a detail which you may see incorrectly, a detail which the expert you observed used as being only incidental to the main fact of the swing.

For example, there are many golfers, and good ones, who appear to drag the clubhead back from the ball. Observing this, you might think it is the key to the proper swing, not realize that it is only a mannerism which has nothing to do with the swing. A drag, in fact, is not a swinging motion.

The imagination constantly communicates information and intelligence to the mind. Most important in gathering such information and intelligence is the sense of sight. Through sight you can detect the physical appearance of the expert's action. But your sense of sight cannot register the feel experienced by the expert while he is wielding the club.

SIGHT too frequently HURTS the golfer, while FEEL ALWAYS HELPS.

I have heard that 85% of knowledge is gained through the sense of sight. But I am sure that the mind of a blind man is not 85% deficient. He develops other senses, notably the sense of feel, to compensate.

Exactly because the sense of sight reveals to the mind more than the other senses, it is also the medium of introducing more interferences and distractions when learning to play. It is sight which spoils your concentration. Try closing your eyes when practicing to learn to sense the feel of swinging the clubhead. Notice that the sense of touch or feel functions better when the sense of sight is shut off.

Fear, or tension, is another mental hazard. Tension is caused by fear. It is fear which creates the wave of panic in the beginner, and prevents him from swinging. When the clubhead is jerked away from the ball, it is fear which forces you to compound your error by trying to hurry the return motion. Thus, you attempt to start your forward swing before even completing the backswing. I use the word "swing" advisedly. Fear causes another common mistake of lifting the club on the back motion and pulling it down.

Some golfers, when that happens, advise you to trust your swing without explaining what the swinging of the clubhead really means. The swing takes a certain measure of time which cannot be hurried. When you bear in mind that the swing is a continuous motion which is felt through the hands and fingers you will not be subject to fears which prevent you from swinging.

Fear may grip you on short iron shots, particularly when attempting to stroke the ball out of a trap. You won't be gripped by that fear when you realize that the principle of the swing is the same for all shots. Failure to appreciate that fact creates the fear of hitting too powerfully. Instead of striking boldly with a swing which follows a shorter arc the shorter the distance, you may lose all feel of the club in your hands and strike ineptly. You may attempt to baby the shot, creating a fluffy motion which carries no control.

There is another mental hazard, that of making mental reservations about accepting statements of facts. You may, at this moment, be experiencing this emotion. It is particularly hard for many players to accept the fact that greater speed and greater accuracy in striking the ball can be developed through swinging than by any other means.

You can, perhaps, learn through visual analysis of the stroke through its various phases. You can eventually piece together the details. This is doing it the hard way. The most dependable route to stroking the ball is through learning to sense a swinging action with the clubhead.

Even the expert at times suffers the mental hazard of trying to inject into the swing more power than he can control. It usually happens when he is being outdriven by his opponent, and the result is the conversion of the application of power from a swing to levering.

You and the expert as well may suffer the mental hazard of worry over the possible outcome of your shot, worry about the danger of a near-by boundary line, the carrying of a hazard, the selection of the proper club.

I offer the same prescription to cure all these ailments of the mind. Learn to settle the issue before starting the stroke. Once you have started the stroke, concentrate only on getting the feel of the swinging action of the clubhead. Learn to swing the clubhead through the medium of your hands and fingers, and eventually you will learn to trust your swing.

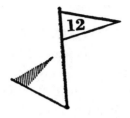

HOW TO BE ACCURATE

ACCURACY MEANS to hit the ball in the direction intended and to make the ball land where it is intended.

To achieve accuracy you must swing the clubhead, with the hands as your medium. When you learn that, you will gain control, which means to have authority of the clubhead, the weapon with which you strike the ball. The swing will give you greater speed and greater accuracy than can any other method.

I shall illustrate by explaining the action of a spinning top. What causes the spinning top to stand on end in defiance of the pull of gravity? Centrifugal force, the rotary, or spinning, motion on a horizontal plane. As long as it is strong enough to resist the pull of gravity, the top will spin. When the rotary force is spent, the top falls on its side.

Notice that the faster the top spins, the steadier is the orbit in which it turns. The top begins to wobble only when the spinning slows down.

The same is true in golf. The greater the speed developed in swinging the clubhead, the steadier and truer will be the orbit in which it swings. No matter how great the speed, a SWINGING ACTION is vital if the club-head is to move in the same path TIME AFTER TIME. Consistent accuracy in wielding the clubhead can be achieved ONLY by the steady, smooth application of power as expressed in a true swing.

You must make that swing a part of your subconscious. Accuracy is impossible when you consciously try to direct the clubhead which is 33 to 43 inches distant from your hands. A variation of 1 degree means the ball will be off line as much as 10 feet when it stops some 200 yards distant. A variation of 3, 4 or 5 degrees compounds the inaccuracy by that many yards.

You cannot achieve accuracy any more than can a baseball pitcher acquire control by thinking of such details as the exact instant at which to release his hold on the ball. A pitcher develops control through a muscular routine which is the result of constant practice. He instinctively releases his grip on the ball, without giving any conscious thought to that detail.

Once you develop a muscular routine founded on swinging the clubhead, you will repeatedly wield it with accuracy. You will also develop as great a speed as your power is capable of producing.

No matter how long you play, however, you will at times give in to the impulse to apply more power than you can control. Invariably, that extra effort will be applied through leverage. It will be force which recedes from the center of the swinging stroke, and it will result in inaccuracy.

When a pitcher loses control he should try to regain his normal movement by throwing rather than by tampering with his method of holding the ball. I was interested in the case of Rex Barney, the Brooklyn Dodgers' pitcher who lost his control and had to be sent to the minor leagues.

Barney had the weapons for greatness, as he proved by pitching a no-hit, no-run masterpiece a few years ago. What happened? If he were a golfer, I think I could have helped him. Obviously, he is attempting the wrong methods of regaining control. Perhaps he is over-concerned with the detail of when to release his hold on the ball. He may be trying to aim the ball at the plate. If he, instead, concentrated on regaining his normal manner of throwing, he might regain his former accuracy.

To assure accuracy in bringing the face of the clubhead against the ball at the proper angle, you must make sure of three things:

1. Check the hold, or grip, on the club. Be sure you are holding the club properly, and in a balanced position.
2. Check your stance. Stand properly in relation to the ball and the direction in which you are aiming. There must be an even distribution of your weight, which assures balance.
3. Swing smoothly and freely.

These are the three factors which determine control. Full control over the club assures accuracy. Control means the ability to feel the head of the club during the swing. When you have that control, you sense what it is doing throughout the action of your swing, making it possible for the face to meet the ball correctly at the moment of impact.

I repeat. You cannot acquire that sense of control if you consciously are aware of other details. Swing the clubhead and forget everything else. Those other actions are purely responsive by-products of the main action of the swing.

Only smooth, easy stroking with a correct grip and stance produces satisfactory distance and accurate direction. It is not some pet device which may be attempted in desperation, nor is it consciously trying to steer for control.

Control automatically results in greater distance. Thus you have the double incentive for developing a correct swing. You will be able to increase the speed of the swing for greater distance, and you also will be accurate in placing the ball where you wish. Need I repeat that the swing is achieved through the continuous action of the hands and fingers?

A moment on the subject of the follow through. Some players appear to be successful although they abruptly halt their swing the moment the club has struck the ball. They are rareties. There are more poor players who do that.

If you carry your swinging action THROUGH the ball, continue it after the impact, you will also get greater speed at the MOMENT of impact. This ultimate in golf stroking will be achieved more easily than if you try to "slug" the ball. Do not do anything to interfere with the swinging action of the clubhead.

The very fact that there are good golfers who differ distinctly in their form is proof that their stroke basically is a swing. How they came to use those mannerisms is immaterial. Jim Ferrier, a great golfer, pronouncedly bends his right knee as he completes his swing. He won the Professional Golfers' Association championship in 1947. That odd mannerism was caused by a knee injury suffered when he played football as a youth in Australia. I have a pupil who plays well in spite of bending his right knee quite pronouncedly. It is caused by a shorter left leg.

There are golfers who assumed certain mannerisms after various experiments. They became convinced it was best for their game. I insist that had those golfers concentrated instead upon correcting their swings, they would have corrected their faults much more easily and with greater success.

The mannerisms resulting from experiments run a wide gamut—change of grip, stance, body adjustment before starting the swing, waggling, etc. Eventually, a temporary solution may be found. Actually, the change may be mildly handicapping. But it brings temporary results because of being a great mental and psychological stimulant. With mind set at ease in the conviction that his new discovery has solved his problem, the player swings more smoothly and steadily, proving the mental point which was the subject of Chapter Eleven.

I knew a businessman who cut seven or eight strokes off his score by playing with a certain famous professional. He followed a simple procedure. On each stroke, the professional took the proper stance, distinctly marking his footprints. Then the businessman stood in his tracks and hit the ball.

This man has been a golfer for many years. It is

ridiculous to think that he hasn't learned how to stand to the ball. But, by standing in the tracks of the professional, his doubts were removed and he was able to concentrate on stroking with a clear mind.

The above is harmless. But there are good golfers who unnecessarily complicate matters by adopting faulty grips or exaggerated stances. Although they may play well for a time, they would play better golf and, above all, BE MORE CONSISTENT IN ATTAINING ACCURACY, if they used sounder methods.

Most unfortunately such golfers, because they may be good, attract imitators who are not good players. For the latter, the adoption of freakish mannerisms is ruinous.

This approach to golf is backing into your task. You concentrate on correcting what is wrong by jumping from the frying pan of one error into the fire of another.

You should from the very beginning learn that which is correct. No matter how hard you work, you are doomed to failure if you attempt any plan which supposes that control can be gained in any way other than by smooth swinging from a sound base.

A leading golf writer once wrote about Bobby Jones: "He trusts his swing to a higher degree than any other golfer I have ever seen. If he is off line on a shot, he may be off 30 yards. Some of the other stars appear to sense that something is wrong, and make at least a partial correction in the hand action as the clubhead is brought against the ball. But once Jones starts his swing, he goes right through with it without any attempt at correction."

112

The great Jones, in short, was primarily concerned with swinging the clubhead, to the exclusion of all distractions. His record proved he was right. He was the only grand slam champion in golf history. He played in eleven U. S. Open championships without once scoring as high as 80.

His record testified to his success in achieving accuracy by striking the ball through trusting his swing, as compared to others who attempted to introduce corrective measures by conscious manipulation while making the stroke.

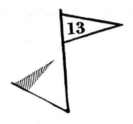

WHY PRACTICE?

WHY PRACTICE? The answer should be obvious. I have insisted from the beginning of this book that good golf is easy to learn. I talked about many factors in learning to play. Yet I rarely strayed from the main thesis, which is the swing.

In Chapter Eight, I wrote:

"A swing is a positive motion. You, to get maximum force, must get all the power you can into that same motion, but without disturbing it, without forcing it from the arc of the swing."

There is but one way to learn how fast you can swing without disturbing the arc. That is through practice.

You learn to swing only through practice. There is no royal road to skill, whether it is golf or any other sport, occupation or avocation. Young children learn to read by repeating over and over and over again the words in their elementary readers.

Big league baseball players already skilled in their profession practice constantly. They practice for more than an hour before each game, shagging flies, throwing by playing catch and taking batting cuts.

114

Tennis players frequently play a set or two before engaging in a match. As for tournament golfers, they practice endless hours. The secret of the success of many weekend amateur golfers is that they practice almost every evening.

If the professionals, the stars in all sports practice constantly, obviously the average golfer needs even more practice, provided it is intelligent practice. The silliest sight in golf is that of people rushing to a golf course, hurrying to the first tee, taking a few swipes at the air, and then starting to play.

I appreciate that many courses, notably public courses, are overcrowded; that courses like Dyker Beach in Brooklyn have no practice tees. You still can engage at least in 15 or 20 minutes of putting practicing, which will help you fall into the rhythm of your swing.

To make permanent progress as a consistent golfer you must accept the golf stroke as a swinging action of the clubhead. I have tried to outline methods of developing that swinging action by teaching you to know it and to identify it by the feel as experienced in the hands. When you understand the swing, you then will have a guide to lead you back to the proper technique whenever your game goes astray.

Once you have learned the art of swinging, the degree of skill you develop will be the result only of your intelligent application of that knowledge through practice. Habit, subconsciously controlled, is the result only of frequent repetition.

The great pianist, Paderewski, once said:

"If I miss one day of practice, I can tell it in my playing. If I miss two days in succession, my critics can tell it. If I miss a week, my audience can tell."

The technique of swinging a golf club is not that fine an art, but practice and skillful play are very definitely intertwined.

Intelligent practice will confirm you in the proper performance of the swing. It will increase the probability that each stroke will approach closer to perfection than the one before.

Constant practice will fix your concentration on the feel of the swinging action of the clubhead. Practice will bring you to the point where your muscular routine will be such that there will be little variation in your swing, no matter how many shots you take. Your swing, of course, must function without conscious interference. Thus, there can be no letup in your effort to keep your conscious mind riveted on sensing the feel of the swing.

It is right practice which gives you form, which is to be distinguished from style. Because of individual mannerisms expert players differ from one another in specific outward appearances. With some golfers these mannerisms, which are incidental to the playing of good golf, are the result of intentionally striving for a certain effort like making a "pretty picture" at the finish of the swing.

These mannerisms serve no purpose other than to distinguish one golfer from another in the same way that people differ in the way they walk. Unfortunately, many golfers stress these to the point where they engage in the confused interplay of the words "style" and "form."

"I cannot understand why Doe plays such terrible golf," you will hear. "He has fine style."

Someone else will say, about another golfer:

"It's a mystery to me how Blow hits a ball so well. He's got the worst form I ever saw on a golf course."

Both are confused. The dictionary says that "form is the established method of expression or practice," while "style is the mode or manner which is deemed elegant, or in accord with a standard; a distinctive or characteristic manner or method."

Form is the capacity for doing something in substantially the same way, over and over and over again. The form or shape of a swing is an arc. An arc is part of a circle and a circle is the most perfect form or shape there is. A circle is perfect form, not style.

If you swing easily, gracefully and in a manner free from appearance of undue effort, you are using good form. Good form is appealing to the eye. Thus, it will improve any style.

Style then, or the lack of it on the golf course, is that which the eye perceives in the performance of others. Form is the manner of developing that performance.

Carried a step further, your form is directed by the sense of feel, and not by sight. Since you have to feel what you are doing, and cannot see it, there is danger in attempting to imitate other golfers.

Your form, the result of constant practice, will produce relatively consistent results regardless of how awkward

117

you are. Style of performance has no relation to those results, except as it indicates good form.

Only form will produce consistency. The better your form, the more consistent will be your golf. And imitation of others cannot possibly help you discover the feel of the action yourself.

Do not, however, go to the opposite extreme and shun watching the expert because you think this will only harm your golf. If done correctly, the expert will help you. Watch him in practice at every opportunity.

In teaching, I sometimes demonstrate the successive stages of the stroke as made by Ben Hogan. I have the pictures in a small booklet, and produce the effect of an actual motion picture of the stroke by flipping the pages between thumb and forefinger.

I make my pupils concentrate only on the movement of the clubhead. They almost immediately notice that the clubhead moves almost as though it were a weight on a string. Within practical limits, that movement is a near-perfect swinging action from first to last.

There is the value in watching the stars. Notice the steady, rhythmic movement of the clubhead. Notice the action of the hands. Forget everything else, the legs, the head, the body. The hands control the club which they hold. Their movement is directed by the central idea of swinging the clubhead. Succeeding movements of the body, the legs, etc., must be responsive to that one idea.

That's a simple idea which makes good golf possible. But—remember—the Hogans, the Sneads and all the other great players practice hour after hour, in spite of the fact that they play much more golf than you or I can ever expect to.

You too must practice, and along sound principles. Merely going through the motion of hitting one golf ball after another accomplishes nothing. If you are hitting improperly, you compound your error by grooving it. You must practice only that stroke which is a swinging action.

If beset by doubts, you must get back to the beginning. Start with a short stroke which requires no conscious turning of the body. Continue it until you are sure of the feel of the clubhead movement. Then you can gradually increase the length of your stroke. If that doesn't help, then follow the practice I recommended early in this book, that of swinging a weight on a string.

Having positively identified the feel of a swing, you will always be able to recognize it. But you will not always be able to swing smoothly, especially after a long layoff. That happens even to the stars.

After Virginia Van Wie had won her third consecutive U. S. Women's championship in October she played no golf until April. Instead, she played some tennis during the fall months. Tennis requires quick application of leverage in many of the strokes.

The first time Miss Van Wie played again, she scored 95. She got into the routine of the swing the second day and scored an 86. By the third day she was in the groove and scored a 74, an improvement of 21 strokes between her first and third rounds.

As she played those three rounds of golf, her single

119

purpose was to school her concentration on thinking only of the feel of the clubhead action. It is her single aim whenever she practices.

If that's good enough for a champion, it should be good enough for the rest of us.

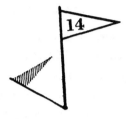

SOME POPULAR FALLACIES

Daryn Hammond wrote:

"Golf is not unlike Cleopatra—age cannot wither her, nor custom stale her infinite variety."

This quotation from the author who has already been quoted several times in this volume is, I think, fitting for this final chapter which I originally had titled "Some Final Observations." You will understand the change in a moment.

I do wish to make the final observation that good golf is simple because you have to learn to do but one thing correctly—swing. The swing will automatically eliminate the faults which beset your game.

I have repeated this so many times that I feel like a nagging wife. But too many people think it incredible that learning can be reduced to such a simple formula. I will agree that it is very elusive. They insist there is much more which must be done.

This is true, particularly, of those who learned the alley cat way, picked up scraps of the food of golfing as they went along. Having suffered the torture of trying to remember a myriad of don'ts as they attempt to hit the ball, they are particularly hard to convince.

They are all confusion. Head down . . . eyes on the ball . . . right elbow in . . . right shoulder down . . . left arm straight . . . stand on your heels . . . pivot . . . etc., etc. No one can do, or think of, all those subjects in the fraction of time between starting and finishing the swing.

When face to face with an individual pupil it is easier to clear up confusion by discovering the cause, or causes, in the particular case. In a general discussion it is impossible to anticipate and discuss separately all likely causes. I shall consider a few of the major difficulties.

I have tried to teach, in addition to the swing, that one can produce greater speed with the clubhead by swinging than by any other means. The story of David and Goliath proves that biblical men understand the advantages of the swinging action as a means of increasing the amount of force with which they could propel an object.

But modern people playing golf find it hard to accept this very simple fact because their experiences come from other fields in which leverage produces the power. Leverage, indispensable for lifting or prying heavy objects, suggests the use of strong leg and body muscles.

Ben Hogan refutes the necessity of strong legs. His legs were weakened considerably by his accident, but his skill wasn't impaired.

The swing is everything. There is no need to exert power, to throw the body weight into the task of swinging the club. You are not trying to lift a stone out of the earth, through the use of a crowbar. Instead of bracing against it, you should treat the ball as though it had no weight.

But even the best golfers have to suppress the eternal impulse to exert more power than can be controlled. Since they are experts, they fall but rarely into that trap. Remember, you can use only as much power as you can control through swinging.

There are many popular fallacies in golf, and most of them are included in the "tips" you have received at one time or another during your ambles along the fairways. Some tips are sound. But since they are drawn from observing the outward, physical motion as the golfer strokes properly, they picture only one phase of that player's action.

Like the fellow who couldn't see the forest for the trees, some experts fail to realize that this one movement they emphasize is a part of the whole action which is entirely responsive to the fundamental process of swinging the clubhead.

It is so with the most popular fallacy of all, that of lifting the head.

When something goes wrong with a shot I blame only one thing—the swing. How often, however, have you topped the ball, after which your foe grins satanically and sings out:

"You peeked."

He implies that you missed because you moved, or lifted your head. I say that you lifted your head BECAUSE you failed to swing properly. I also say that it

123

is impossible to anchor your head, and still hit the ball well.

The head MUST move when you take a full swing. It cannot remain rigidly immobile. The position of the head, however, establishes balance when addressing the ball and before beginning the stroke. When maintaining that easy balance throughout the stroke, the position of the head changes slightly. BUT IT CHANGES.

Too many golfers concentrate so hard on fixing the head rigidly that they fail to concentrate on the fundamental of swinging the clubhead. What you do with the head when you are swinging properly requires no conscious thought. The head takes care of itself when you concentrate on swinging the clubhead.

It is the same with keeping your eye on the ball. Of course you look at an object when you are trying to strike it. I pity your fingers if you attempt to drive a nail into a board with your eyes closed. Your eyes are your guide in striking a golf ball just as they are in every other sport. But you do not have to make a ceremony out of looking at the ball, by holding your head still.

If you are swinging properly there will be no tendency to shift your gaze elsewhere. Only uncertainty will force your eyes to shift. When you are in doubt, you tend to lift your head. That's why there is more head-lifting when trying to hit out of a trap than off the tee.

If you worry about a bunker, a slice or a hook when in the act of swinging, you will be overwhelmed by an impulse to look and see what happens as a result of your stroke. Because your attention is not on sensing the feel of swinging the clubhead the very result you fear may be the outcome.

I can elaborate on many more details which are the subjects of common discussion. But I think I have made it clear in this book that my method of teaching avoids the "don'ts" of golf. I have no concern with "don't lift your head" or the many other don'ts, from overswinging to bending the left arm.

For example, that stiff left arm about which you hear so much. If you kept that arm truly stiff, something would have to give when you attempted to swing. It might be the arm. Then you would be wearing a cast while watching other people golf. A proper swing will take care of the arm; it will take care of the pivot. It will take care of everything, including the head and the eyes. Remember you cannot do more than one thing at a time.

So I repeat again what I said at the beginning of this book. There is only one perfect way to strike a golf ball. That is by swinging the clubhead. You swing the clubhead with your hands and fingers. You sense the feel of the swing through your hands and fingers. Your hands are everything in this business of playing good golf easily.

As Walt Whitman wrote about women, I say about the golf swing:

I will elude you, even though you thought you
    had unquestionably caught me.
Behold, you see I have already escaped from you.

But, remember:

125

Truth at first is derided, then debated.
And at last accepted as a matter of course.

So go to it.
SWING THE CLUBHEAD.

Other Titles from
Echo Point Books
You May Enjoy

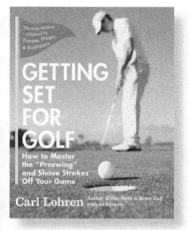

Getting Set for Golf
by Carl Lohren

PGA Tour Pro Carl Lohren follows up his blockbuster book *One Move To Better Golf* with tips and techniques to transform yourself from duffer to scratch golfer. In print large enough to read with a golf club in your hands, Lohren teaches how to master the "preswing" and visualize your way to a better overall game.

HARDCOVER ISBN 978-1-62654-502-1

Paul Runyan's Book for Senior Golfers

Paul Runyan's Book for Senior Golfers is crammed with unique direction about putting, chipping, and making wedge shots from long grass around greens. This book features helpful instructional line drawings and photographs, as well as tips on training and the proper competitive attitude. Because of Runyan's sound instructional technique, younger players will also find this book useful.

PAPERBACK ISBN 978-1-62654-840-4
HARDCOVER ISBN 978-1-62654-050-7

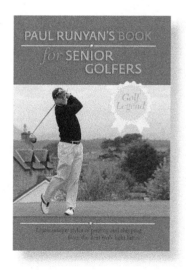

Our books may be ordered from any bookstore or online purveyor of books, or directly through our Web site, www.echopointbooks.com. Or visit our retail store, located in Brattleboro, Vermont.

CPSIA information can be obtained
at www.ICGtesting.com
Printed in the USA
BVHW041415171019
561378BV00008B/247/P